# D. H. Lawrence and Tradition

# D. H. Lawrence and Tradition

*edited by* JEFFREY MEYERS

The University of Massachusetts Press
Amherst, 1985

*Copyright © 1985 by Jeffrey Meyers*

*All rights reserved
First published in the USA in 1985
by The University of Massachusetts Press*

ISBN 0-87023-464-1

**Library of Congress Cataloging in Publication Data**
Main entry under title:

D. H. Lawrence and tradition.

  Bibliography: p.
  Includes index.
  1. Lawrence, D. H. (David Herbert), 1885–1930—
Knowledge—Literature—Addresses, essays, lectures.
2. Literature—19th century—History and criticism—
Addresses, essays, lectures.  3. Influence (Literary,
artistic, etc.)—Addresses, essays, lectures.  I. Meyers,
Jeffrey.  II. Title: D. H. Lawrence and tradition.
PR6023.A93Z623383   1985      823'.912      84-16175
ISBN 0-87023-464-1

*Typeset by Spire Print Services Ltd, Salisbury
Printed in Great Britain by Paradigm Print, Bungay*

# Contents

*Notes on the Contributors*

| | | | |
|---|---|---|---|
| | Introduction | *Jeffrey Meyers* | 1 |
| 1 | Lawrence and Blake | *John Colmer* | 9 |
| 2 | Lawrence and Carlyle | *Paul Delany* | 21 |
| 3 | Lawrence and Ruskin: The Sage as Word-Painter | *George P. Landow* | 35 |
| 4 | Lawrence and George Eliot: The Genesis of *The White Peacock* | *H.M. Daleski* | 51 |
| 5 | Lawrence and Hardy | *Robert Langbaum* | 69 |
| 6 | Whitman and the Poetics of Lawrence | *Roberts W. French* | 91 |
| 7 | Lawrence and the Nietzschean Matrix | *Kingsley Widmer* | 115 |

*Notes*     132

*Index*     151

For Donald Baker

# Notes on the Contributors

JOHN COLMER was educated at Oxford and has taught at the Universities of Khartoum, Birmingham and Adelaide, where he is the Jury Professor of English. He has published widely on the Romantic poets, and is the author of *Coleridge: Critic of Society* (1959), *Approaches to the Novel* (1967), *E. M. Forster: The Personal Voice* (1975) and *Coleridge to "Catch-22": Images of Society* (1978), which contains a discussion of Lawrence's social thought. He has also edited *Church and State* (1976) for the *Collected Coleridge*, and three anthologies of poetry: *New Choice*, *Mainly Modern* and *Pattern and Voice*.

H. M. DALESKI is Professor of English at the Hebrew University, Jerusalem, and author of *The Forked Flame: A Study of D. H. Lawrence* (1965), *Dickens and the Art of Analogy* (1970), *Joseph Conrad: The Way of Dispossession* (1977) and *The Divided Heroine: A Recurrent Pattern in Six English Novels* (1983).

PAUL DELANY is Professor of English at Simon Fraser University, and author of *British Autobiography in the Seventeenth Century* (1969) and *D. H. Lawrence's Nightmare: The Writer and his Circle in the Years of the Great War* (1978).

ROBERTS W. FRENCH is Professor of English at the University of Massachusetts. He has written on Whitman for the *Walt Whitman Review*, and other essays have appeared in *College English*, *The Nation*, *Milton Quarterly* and the *Massachusetts Review*.

GEORGE P. LANDOW is Professor of English at Brown University, and author of *The Aesthetic and Critical Theories of John Ruskin* (1971), *Holman Hunt and Typological Symbol* (1979), *Victorian Types, Victorian Shadows* (1980) and *Images of Crisis: Literary Iconology, 1750 to the Present* (1982).

ROBERT LANGBAUM is James Branch Cabell Professor of English and American Literature at the University of Virginia, and author of *The Poetry of Experience* (1963), *The Modern Spirit* (1970) and *Isak Dinesen's Art* (1975). His latest book—*The Mysteries of Identity: A*

*Theme in Modern Literature* (1977), reissued in paperback in 1982 — deals extensively with Lawrence.

JEFFREY MEYERS is Professor of English at the University of Colorado. He is author of twenty books on modern literature, including several works on T. E. Lawrence and George Orwell, biographies of Katherine Mansfield (1978) and Wyndham Lewis (1980), *Wyndham Lewis: A Revaluation* (1980), *Fiction and the Colonial Experience* (1973), *Painting and the Novel* (1975), *A Fever at the Core* (1976), *Married to Genius* (1977), *Homosexuality and Literature* (1977), *Hemingway: The Critical Heritage* (1982), *D. H. Lawrence and the Experience of Italy* (1982) and *Disease and the Novel, 1880–1960* (1985).

KINGSLEY WIDMER has taught comparative literature at ten institutions in both America and Europe, and is now Professor of English at San Diego State University. He has published social criticism and poetry as well as many literary-cultural studies, including *D. H. Lawrence: The Art of Perversity* (1962), *Henry Miller* (1963), *The Literary Rebel* (1965), *The Ways of Nihilism: Melville's Short Novels* (1970), *The End of Culture* (1973), *Paul Goodman* (1980) and *The Edges of Extremity* (1980).

# Introduction

## JEFFREY MEYERS

> To have gathered from the air a live tradition
> or from a fine old eye the unconquered flame
> This is not vanity.
> Pound, *Cantos*, LXXXI

> One must keep up tradition.
> Lawrence, *Lady Chatterley's Lover*

T. S. Eliot believed the writer's grasp of tradition derived from his sense of history:

> The historical sense involves a perception, not only of the pastness of the past, but of its presence; the historical sense compels a man to write not merely with his own generation in his bones, but with a feeling that the whole of the literature of Europe from Homer and within it the whole of the literature of his own country has a simultaneous existence and composes a simultaneous order. This historical sense . . . is what makes a writer traditional. And it is at the same time what makes a writer most acutely conscious of his place in time, of his own contemporaneity.[1]

Eliot's concept of tradition was based on a body of literature whose form and meaning persist, as it is absorbed by the writers of succeeding generations. Yet Eliot could not see that Lawrence was precisely that kind of traditional writer.

In *After Strange Gods* (1934) Eliot asserted: "Lawrence started life wholly free from any restriction of tradition or institution . . . [and suffered from a] lack of intellectual and social training." He emphasized Lawrence's "incapacity for what we ordinarily call thinking" and categorized him as "a very sick man indeed."[2] In 1951 Eliot claimed: "Lawrence was an ignorant man in the sense that he was unaware of how much he did not know."[3] Eliot, whose judgments were based on appalling ignorance about Lawrence's nonconformist background, education, intellectual interests, artistry and place in the European intellectual tradition, assumed the double snobbery of an American outsider in English society and of an Anglo-Catholic toward the literary tradition of the Dissenting church.[4] Iris Murdoch, who quotes Eliot's statement: "neither Shakespeare nor Dante did any real thinking,"[5] calls Eliot's remark about Lawrence's intellect "an astonishing judgment. Whatever *is* thinking if Lawrence couldn't think?"[6]

F. R. Leavis challenged Eliot's view in *For Continuity* (1933) and convincingly maintained: "In our time, when the gap in continuity is almost complete, [Lawrence] may be said to represent, concretely in his living person, the essential human tradition."[7] Leavis continued to explain Lawrence's transmission of a social and spiritual heritage in *The Great Tradition* (1948) and in *D. H. Lawrence: Novelist* (1955), which reprinted his rebuttal of Eliot's prejudices and his insistence that "Lawrence *was* brought up in an environment of a living and central tradition."

> He had a better education, one better calculated to develop his genius for its most fruitful use, than any other he could have got. ... The Chapel, in the Lawrence circle, was the centre of a strong social life, and the focus of a still persistent cultural tradition that had as its main drive the religious tradition of which Mr. Eliot is so contemptuous. To turn, as Lawrence did, the earnestness and moral seriousness of that tradition to the powering of a strenuous intellectual inquiringness was all in the tradition.[8]

Recent criticism has opposed Eliot's and Leavis' idea of a nourishing tradition and emphasized the inhibiting and suffocating aspects of literary influence, which lead to imitation, parody, pastiche, plagiarism or paralysis. Anna Balakian claims: "Often the influences of authors of the same nationality and language upon each other are negative influences, the result of reactions, for generations often tend to be rivals of each other and in the name of individualism reject in the work of their elders what they consider to be the conventions of the past."[9] Walter Jackson Bate's *The Burden of the Past* quotes one of Johnson's remarks about politics in *The Rambler* (No.

86) and then applies it to literature: "It is, indeed, always *dangerous* to be placed in a state of unavoidable comparison with excellence, and the danger is still greater when that excellence is consecrated by death." Bate stresses the deepening self-consciousness, loss of self-confidence and accumulating anxiety when authors competitively confront the literary legacy of the past. Bate believes the modern artist is faced with an overwhelming question: *"What is there left to do?"*[10] But Lawrence, who wrote distinctively on an enormous range of subjects—literature, art, religion, philosophy, psychology, anthropology and education—was not seriously troubled by this problem.

Harold Bloom's *The Anxiety of Influence*—strongly influenced by Bate—gives Bate's argument a Freudian (even Darwinian) interpretation, introduces some typically obscure terminology and insists that strong poets, in quest of new literary territory, misread "one another, so as to clear imaginative space. . . . Figures of capable imagination appropriate for themselves. But nothing is got for nothing, and self-appropriation involves the immense anxieties of indebtedness, for what strong maker desires the realization that he failed to create himself?"[11] Bloom, who places Lawrence among the "great deniers of influence," is effectively refuted by the overwhelming evidence of *D. H. Lawrence and Tradition*.

The seven chapters in this book show how Lawrence interprets, revalues, absorbs and transforms the work of Blake, Carlyle, Ruskin, George Eliot, Hardy, Whitman and Nietzsche. Though the critics differ in their approach to the question of Lawrence's relation to tradition and receptivity to influence, they all assume that his use of the style, forms and ideas of his predecessors is positive. They believe that Lawrence's fiction, poetry and criticism derive their resonance, meaning and value—and much of their inspiration—from his vital connection to significant authors of the nineteenth century.

Lawrence was influenced by a great many factors: his origins, family and religion;[12] his conversation, education and reading;[13] his friends, lovers and wife; his moral, social and intellectual milieu; his travels, poverty and illness. This book concerns the literary influence of seven major writers on the attitude, sensibility, style, structure, tone, theme and technique of Lawrence's work.[14] The concept of influence encompasses aesthetics, psychology and philosophy as well as literary history and provides, as Haskell Bloch observes, "insight into the aesthetic character of individual works and at the same time clarifies and defines their historical relationships"; it offers a kind of double vision and illuminates "both the individuality and the interrelatedness of literary works."[15] Ihab Hassan agrees with Eliot and with Bloch that the study of "multiple correlations and multiple similarities functioning in a historical sequence," of the artist's relation to the particular traditions of the past and the modification of one tradition into another, "defines the individual aspects of his work."[16]

*D. H. Lawrence and Tradition* could have contained additional chapters on Lawrence's relation to the style and thought of the Bible; Wordsworth and the concept of nature; Keats and Byron as letter-writers; the Brontës and passion; Dickens, Bennett and urban realism; Edward Carpenter and homosexuality; Cooper and the American Indian; Melville and Stevenson as travel writers; Verga and primitivism; Tolstoy and the idea of love; Freud and German literature; Renaissance and modern painting.[17] But an emphasis on the most dominant influences in Lawrence's intellectual background provides a more powerful and persuasive argument.

In *D. H. Lawrence and the Experience of Italy* I briefly mentioned the influence of Ruskin, Hardy, Whitman and Nietzsche. Mellors' scheme for rebirth and plea for men who could sing and swagger and wear bright red trousers as a way to replace money with manhood has deep roots in the regenerative idealism of Ruskin. In Hardy as in Lawrence's *The Rainbow*, the characters have a strong family bond, a sense of the rural community, an organic relation to the eternal round of the seasons and a connection to the landscape which seems to exist as an independent force. Lawrence's poetic style changes from the traditional form of the early poems written under the influence of the Georgians to the loose, long-lined doctrinal assertions in the mode of Walt Whitman. And the Labour leader Willie Struthers, like his ideological adversary Kangaroo, wants to base his political movement on Whitman's democratic-homosexual love of man for man. The most powerful onslaught against St Paul's deviation from the Gospels, Nietzsche's *The Antichrist* (1888), condemns, with the passionate rhetoric that Lawrence would later adopt in *The Man Who Died*, the degeneration of God into a force that opposed human life.

But the authoritative contributions and concerted effort in *D. H. Lawrence and Tradition* are better suited to this immense and important subject, for no single scholar has the breadth of knowledge to draw together all the complex connections between Lawrence and the masters of the previous century. This book heightens our appreciation and comprehension of Lawrence by revealing many echoes and allusions to earlier works, by suggesting the richness and depth in the texture of his art, and by providing a cultural context in which to read Lawrence's works. Lawrence has also influenced our understanding and response to nineteenth-century authors through his criticism of Hardy and American literature as well as by his creative work; he has taught us to see these authors through his eyes and to read them as he did.

*D. H. Lawrence and Tradition* explores the very roots of Lawrence's art, for tradition is the cultural equivalent of the individual consciousness. This study examines Lawrence's lively intellectual response to writers who showed him new directions and gave him a sense of freedom. It reveals where he comes from and where he is going, how he fulfills the implications and completes the potential of his Romantic and Victorian forebears, and how, by rewriting the works of others, he makes them entirely his own. Though Lawrence transcends any single literary influence, part of his receptive genius is the ability to select and learn from the traditions of the past. He had the persistence and courage to continue his struggle with the potent dead and, from this spiritual combat, to recreate a new art. Lawrence's exploration of earlier writers and cultivation of underlying temperamental and stylistic affinities lead him to self-discovery. His debts to tradition enhance rather than diminish his originality and establish him more seriously as a writer of the first rank.

Despite the apparently rival claims for pre-eminent influence, the diverse approaches of the seven critics present a remarkably unified and coherent view of Lawrence's complex relation to the past. Lawrence shares with most of the writers from Blake to Nietzsche a close connection to the line of Protestant Dissent; a belief in Darwinism; a plea for an organic as opposed to a mechanistic society; an emotional and spontaneous style; an immediacy, intensity and vitality; fictional characters rooted in the landscape; the quest of superior female characters for an appropriate mate; an awareness of unconscious motivation; an emphasis on the physical body and sexual being; a belief in the redeeming power of sexual love (for sex was the essential problem of the post-war generation as religion was of the Victorians); and a prophetic and apocalyptic vision. This book also reveals how Lawrence subtly absorbs what he can use from his principal models and then diverges from their conventions and their influence. George P. Landow notes that Lawrence sometimes rejects his predecessor's ideas or formulates his own in direct reaction to them and that his secularized, ironic allusions to specific biblical texts subvert the traditional interpretations.

The contributors focus on different but complementary aspects of Lawrence's major works and provide a full account of his literary career. H. M. Daleski deals with *The White Peacock* and *Sons and Lovers*, Roberts W. French with *Look! We Have Come Through!* and the poems of death, George P. Landow with *Twilight in Italy* and *Sea and Sardinia*, Robert Langbaum with the *Study of Thomas Hardy* and *The Rainbow*, Kingsley Widmer with the stories and the leadership novels, Paul Delany with *Women in Love* and *The Plumed Serpent*, John Colmer with the poetry and *Lady Chatterley's Lover*.

John Colmer sees Blake as a liberating (not an inhibiting) influence, as a passionate revolutionary who shows the way to a new kind of instant poetry of the sheer present. "What Lawrence found in Blake," writes Colmer, "was a poet inspired by a prophetic and apocalyptic vision, whose response to life was immediate, urgent and unconventional. He found a congenial sensibility for whom everything in life was Holy, a sensibility out of harmony with the materialism of the age, an imagination whose natural tendency was to reverse or invert the values of established religion and social propriety."

Paul Delany quotes Lawrence's remark: "We have to hate our immediate predecessors, to get free from their authority," and makes the crucial point (which refutes Balakian's claim) that "Lawrence saw the major Victorians as much less intrusive rivals than the established writers of his own era." Delany notes that both Lawrence and Carlyle had common roots in British puritanism and German idealist philosophy, and that both saw sex as subversive to social hierarchies. Delany shows the similarity of their political views, personal temperament and prose style.

George P. Landow concentrates on the stylistic techniques that Lawrence learned from Ruskin: the transformation of visually oriented prose "into symbolic or mythological set-pieces" in his novels and travel books. Landow concludes that both men shared an Evangelical Protestant tradition, were (like Blake) practicing artists and writers, and became controversial critics of art and society: "Lawrence's desire to combine the techniques and interests of the word-painter with the mission of the secular prophet makes him, however unexpectedly, a Ruskinian modernist."

H. M. Daleski focuses on the genesis of *The White Peacock* and argues that the novel "may rewardingly be read as Lawrence's rewriting of *The Mill on the Floss*." Daleski remarks: "It is in his having gone beyond George Eliot in his first novel that Lawrence may be said to have found himself through her—to have discovered . . . the basic thematic material which he was steadily to mine" in *Sons and Lovers, The Rainbow, Women in Love* and *Lady Chatterley's Lover*.

Robert Langbaum concentrates on Lawrence's *Study of Thomas Hardy*, in which he rewrites Hardy's novels, as he rewrote George Eliot's, turning them into Lawrencean novels and thus making a bridge between Hardy and himself. Langbaum reveals that Lawrence took from Hardy several basic ideas about sexual identity and the relation of men and women, and learned from the Victorian novelist to set up highly concentrated scenes that permit the explosive revelation of internal states of being.

Roberts W. French shows that Whitman gave Lawrence a sense of integrity and artistic freedom; that they shared similar attitudes to the body, sex and death. French states that Lawrence's *Apocalypse* expresses the essential themes he shared with Whitman: "the mysterious beauty of life in a physical world . . . the inescapable bonds of the human community; the merging of the one in the many; the organic relationships connecting all that exists."

Kingsley Widmer, in characteristically combative style, surveys the various Lawrencean traditions and demonstrates Lawrence's intellectual relation to Nietzsche through his early education and Frieda's ideological enthusiasm. Widmer analyzes how Nietzsche's concept of the Will functions in *Women in Love* and the leadership novels; and shows, through their striking similarities, how "the Nietzschean provides a locus for the attack on prevailing values, the efforts at 'transvaluation,' and the dramaturgy of demystification of a nihilistic age."

Just as Thomas Mann was nourished, stimulated and inspired by the influence of Goethe, Schopenhauer, Wagner, Nietzsche and Freud; T. S. Eliot by Dante, Webster, Donne, Laforgue and Pound; and Hemingway by Tolstoy, Kipling, Crane, Joyce and T. E. Lawrence, so D. H. Lawrence dynamically transforms the English, American and German literary traditions. Lawrence's work, like T. S. Eliot's, represents a humane continuity between past and present. His art develops tradition, recognizes sympathetic temperaments in past writers, and discovers in them forms of expression that can be reaffirmed and recreated.[18]

CHAPTER ONE

# Lawrence and Blake

## JOHN COLMER

The affinity between Lawrence and Blake has frequently been noticed. In an essay on Lawrence in *For Continuity* (1933), F. R. Leavis wrote that the "community between Blake's and Lawrence's preoccupations is obvious: they might both be said to have been concerned with the vindication of impulse and spontaneity against 'reason' and convention."[1] Since Leavis's seminal remarks few writers on Lawrence have failed to comment on the connection. Harry T. Moore's statement in *The Life and Works of D. H. Lawrence* in 1951 that "Blake's so-called 'immoralism,' his cultivated primitivism, and his political libertarianism make him seem a definite ancestor of Lawrence" summarises the parallels most often noted.[2] But apart from the brief essays by Kerker Quinn and Constantine Stavrou,[3] no one has taken up the original challenge implicit in Leavis's discussion in *For Continuity*: "Blake's name suggests itself for this comparison because there is between him and Lawrence a significant parallel which might be worked out in detail."[4]

The following account is an attempt to explore some of the parallels in greater detail than before and to consider whether it is possible to advance from talk of "affinities" and "parallels" to a definition of anything that could be called a shared tradition. At first sight no single tradition might seem broad enough to include two such eccentric figures of genius; and, in any case, the whole idea of tradition and influence is undergoing such a process of radical questioning and reassessment as the result of the work of Harold Bloom and others that any conclusions reached in this sphere must remain tentative and problematic. Moreover, it is worth bearing in mind from the outset Eugene Goodheart's warning that "the unfortunate effect of underlining Lawrence's debts to tradition is that it tends to deprive him of the special claim that he makes upon us."[5] Equally salutary is Kerker Quinn's reminder that even if Lawrence does refer to Blake approvingly he also "derives a great deal from Nietzsche, from Whitman, from Freud, all of whom write similarly to Blake without realising it," and that because "the threads of influence are hopelessly tangled," we should speak of "the *relationship* of Blake to Lawrence" and not of influence, which can neither be isolated nor measured.[6]

Both Blake and Lawrence were painter-poets. The creator of the embryonic artist Paul Morel in *Sons and Lovers* recognised the affinity with Blake early and cast Jessie Chambers, the original of Miriam, in the role of his artist wife-companion. In *D. H. Lawrence: A Personal Record*, Jessie Chambers describes a meeting with Lawrence in Hythe Park Wood in snowdrop time.

> As we walked through the wood he talked to me in his rapt way about Blake, telling me what a wonderful man he was, quite poor, who taught himself everything he knew; how he made pictures and wrote poems that were interdependent, and did the printing and engraving himself, in fact producing the book entirely by his own hands. He told me that Blake's wife was a poor girl whom he taught to read, and also to print and engrave, and what a marvellous helpmate she was to him. . . . For a little time we lived with Blake and his wife.
>
> When we went in the house, fresh from the crisp air, Lawrence's face eager with talking, my father laughed at us, but my thoughts were with William Blake and his wife.[7]

For Lawrence the process of identification was close, intense and wide-ranging; it was not a matter of passing admiration or temporary imitation of a literary style. In Blake the young Lawrence recognised a fellow spirit, a poor, self-educated man of genius who united the arts of poetry and painting in a highly individual manner, someone who was isolated from society and established cultural traditions but dependent for support on his loving wife. For the Nottinghamshire miner's son Blake was an exemplary liberating influence.

At this early stage in Lawrence's career knowledge of Blake's biography probably came from Gilchrist's *Life* with its telling anecdotes and liberal quotations, but there is nothing to suggest that the process that Jessie referred to as living "with Blake and his wife" involved the kind of naked Garden of Eden episode chronicled by

Gilchrist.[8] Both Lawrence and Jessie were still sufficiently influenced by the strict nonconformist ethos in which they were brought up to find many aspects of Blake's life and work a daring challenge to accepted Christian ethics and late Victorian propriety. Lawrence even forbad Jessie to read Emily Brontë at this time. The work of Blake that they knew best was the *Songs;* and, in a passage describing Lawrence's gift of Shelley and *The Rubaiyat* Jessie records that in exchange she "gave him Blake's *Songs of Innocence and Songs of Experience*." The longer works, including the Prophetic Books, Lawrence could have encountered in extract in Gilchrist or in the numerous critical works on Blake that marked the turn of the century interest in the neglected visionary poet.[9] The earliest reference to Blake in Lawrence's fiction occurs in chapter 3 of *The White Peacock*. In later life he almost certainly expanded his knowledge of Blake's poetry, so that the passage in Huxley's *Point Counter Point* that describes Mark Rampion's experience in all probability comes close to expressing Lawrence's mature estimate.

"I've been re-reading Blake," he said. And he began to speak about the *Marriage of Heaven and Hell*.

"Blake was civilized," he insisted, "*civilized*." Civilization is harmony and completeness. Reason, feeling, instinct, the life of the body—Blake managed to include and harmonize everything. Barbarism is being lop-sided. You can be a barbarian of the intellect as well as of the body. You can be a barbarian of the soul and the feelings as well as of sensuality. Christianity made us barbarians of the soul and now science is making us barbarians of the intellect. Blake was the last civilized man.[10]

A year before Lawrence's death, the official protectors of civilisation by an odd irony of fate cast Lawrence and Blake in the role of obscene corruptors of public morals. At the exhibition of Lawrence's twenty-five paintings at the Warren Gallery in London between June and July 1929, the police impounded thirteen of Lawrence's paintings, seized four copies of the Mandrake Press book of reproductions of the paintings and temporarily impounded Blake's *Pencil Drawings* as obscene. Thus, both at the beginning and the end of Lawrence's artistic career, the figure of Blake figures prominently in the story.

Lawrence's direct imitations of Blake's poetry are neither very significant nor successful. There is, for example, the poem "Michael

Angelo," said by Helen Corke to have been written after a visit to the Tate Gallery but which was more likely inspired by a reproduction of Michelangelo's *The Creation of Adam* in the Sistine chapel. The early printed version of this poem in *Love Poems and Others* (1913) is Blakean only in its expression of sacred awe before the mystery of creation. The later expanded text recasts the experience in a series of rhetorical questions reminiscent of Blake's "The Tyger."

> Who shook thy roundness in his finger's cup?
> Who sunk his hands in firmness down his sides
> And drew the circle of his grasp, O man,
> Along thy limbs delighted as a bride's?

The imitation is a failure, as F. B. Pinion comments, largely because of Lawrence's proneness to explain, the extreme vagueness of the end of the poem and the "rhyme-determined factitiousness which lacks the clarity of the original."[11] The same critic notes that in the poem "The Ass" the combination of seriousness and humour reminds one of "some hairy horned God the Father in a William Blake Imagination."[12] He also points out that the best text for Lawrence's dramatic sketch "New Eve and Old Adam" is to be found in Blake's "The Clod and the Pebble." For his "Baby poem" called "Ten Months Old," Lawrence specifically referred Blanche Jennings to a poem by Meredith and also to the opening lines of Blake's "Infant Joy."[13]

Lawrence's debt to Blake as a poet is not to be measured by such relatively trivial similarities and parallels between individual poems, for he owed little to Blake in the matter of technique. It is more appropriately gauged, as the editors of Lawrence's *Complete Poems* have pointed out, if we see the Blake of the *Songs of Experience* and the Wordsworth of "Resolution and Independence" as the prophets of the new kind of poetry that Lawrence was to describe as "instant poetry ... the unrestful, ungraspable poetry of the sheer present, poetry whose permanence lies in its windlike transit."[14] What Lawrence found in Blake was a poet inspired by a prophetic and apocalyptic vision, whose response to life was immediate, urgent and unconventional. He found a congenial sensibility for whom everything in life was Holy, a sensibility out of harmony with the materialism of the age, an imagination whose natural tendency was to reverse or invert the values of established religion and social propriety. Blake's insight into the unity of all creation, his vindication of the wisdom of the body and his creation of a highly individual style unfettered by the conventional restraints of regular metre and poetic diction, "an organic or expressive form to express his naked, passionate experience,"[15] served as a permanent source of inspiration for Lawrence. Consequently, Lawrence's most Blakean poems are those that celebrate the instinctive energies of animals and man and the highly cryptic, idiosyncratic poems in *Pansies*. The opening lines of "Obscenity," for instance, have the condensed paradoxical power of Blake's proverbs in *The Marriage of Heaven and Hell*; "The body of itself is clean, but the caged mind is a sewer inside, it pollutes, O it pollutes."

Yet, when all these connections and debts have been noted, the truth is that Blake's inspiration and influence is more strongly felt in Lawrence's prose than in his verse. Significantly, all five of the Blakean passages that Leavis quotes in his essay on Lawrence in *For Continuity* come from Lawrence's prose. Leavis selected such obvious passages as the two from "The Crown": the one beginning "It is wrong to make the lion lie down with the lamb" and the other "But it is the fight of opposites which is holy." He also quoted the description of the tiger as a "fanged and brindled Holy Ghost," from "Aristocracy" and the passage "The sun, I tell you is alive, and more alive than I am, or a tree ... it is the Holy Ghost in full raiment, shaking and walking, alive as a tiger is, only more so," from the same essay.[16] The Blakean verbal echoes are certainly strong, but if we look for something more radical than reminiscent phrase and similarity of sentiment it is to be found most clearly in Lawrence's essay "The Two Principles."[17] There the affirmation that "Life can never be produced or made," that it is "an unbroken oneness, indivisible," that it "depends on duality and polarity" and that "fourfold activity is the root-activity of the universe" brings together in a single developing argument the main substance of Blake's personal system. This affirmation rests firmly on the doctrine formulated in *The Marriage of Heaven and Hell* that "without contraries is no progression" and the idea that it is necessary for man to develop the fourfold vision in order to escape imprisonment in a mechanistic universe of single vision and Newton's sleep.[18] Like Blake, Lawrence sees the senses as the five portals of the soul. As he says in the essay "The Two Principles," "through the gates of the eyes and nose and mouth and ears, through the delicate parts of the fingers, through the great windows of the yearning breast, we pass into our oneness with the universe, and the great extension of being toward infinitude."[19]

Although Lawrence's style is deeply rooted in the Bible, it cannot be claimed as it has been of Blake that his life-long mission was to reinterpret Christianity in order to free it from worldly accretions, to disengage it from the hypocrisies of society and the vested interests of an established church. Although Lawrence's arrogance and sectarian zeal probably owed much to his Congregational upbringing, he made an early break with institutionalised Christianity of any sort and spent the rest of his life searching the world for a more imaginative and satisfying religion or, as in the case of *The Plumed Serpent*, seeking to create a new one from primitive Aztec myths. Nevertheless, he retained a strong nostalgia for communal hymn-singing and a retentive memory for biblical cadence and phrase; he also retained certain apocalyptic modes of thought and expression. Graham Hough's suggestion that Lawrence's basically naturalistic philosophy is masked by his use of biblical language ignores the extent to which his whole world view was shaped by boyhood grounding in the Bible.[20] The structure continued to be apocalyptic but ceased to be Christian. Blake wished to save Christianity from the Churches; Lawrence sought to save men from Christianity itself. It could hardly be otherwise when what he was most intent on creating was his own religion, based on the wisdom of the body and the principle of polarity, or if not quite creating a religion of his own, at least charting an alternative secular path to salvation.

Lawrence belongs to a visionary, apocalyptic tradition quite as obviously as Blake and there are remarkable similarities in the way the two writers develop their regenerative visions through heightened biblical rhythms, poetic metaphors and myths. Although the novelist found it unnecessary to create a wholly independent personal mythology in order to avoid political censorship and to body forth his system, as Blake did in the Prophetic Books, his imagination was naturally mythopoeic; it seized on congenial myths from a great variety of cultures, Greek, Etruscan, Roman and Aztec. These he refashioned and made his own, as in his idiosyncratic rehandling of the Christ myth in *The Man Who Died* or in his creation of a new religion, Quetzalcoatl, from Aztec sources, in the *The Plumed Serpent*, where his memories of Congregational hymns enables him to create a seemingly authentic hymnology for the new religion.

Related to this visionary mode in both writers was an all-pervasive strain of anti-rationalism. For both writers, exclusive trust in reason was wholly sterile, yet both accepted that a tension between opposites was necessary for any healthy development. Thus in considering the relation between reason and emotion, Lawrence wrote: "Emotions by themselves become just a nuisance. The mind by itself becomes a sterile thing, making everything sterile.... You've got to marry the pair of them. Apart they are no good." In spite of this formal recognition that extremes meet and are necessary, no ideal of temperate wholeness can account for the apocalyptic fervour in much of Blake's and Lawrence's writings. This springs from the sense of an indwelling divinity which is the source of transcendent visions and the missionary urge to communicate inspired truths. There is a striking parallel between a passage in Lawrence's *The Plumed Serpent:* "And there God is; and Paradise; inside the hearts of living men and women" and Blake's "All deities reside in the human breast." From this sense of an indwelling spirit arises an unquestioning confidence, a proud certainty that is the reverse of Christian humility; this is evident in Blake's belief that "God wants not Man to Humble himself" and Lawrence's "Humility is a sin against the Holy Ghost."[21]

For both writers the regeneration of the individual society involves a passionate rejection of authoritarian restraint and an invitation to live more fully through the imagination and the senses. In the main two views have been taken about the tradition to which Lawrence's social criticism belongs. The majority view, conveniently represented by Raymond Williams, places him firmly in the tradition created by Coleridge, Carlyle, Arnold and Ruskin, an anti-mechanistic tradition that considered the industrial revolution responsible for most of society's ills and which offered as an alternative some kind of return to the organic community. There is abundant evidence in the novels for such a placing of Lawrence, ranging from the treatment of the Crich family in *Women in Love* to the oft-quoted passage from *Lady Chatterley's Lover* that ends: "The industrial England blots out the agricultural England. One meaning blots out another. The new England blots out the old England. And the continuity is not organic, but mechanic."[22]

The antithesis in the last sentence would seem to locate Lawrence firmly in the tradition identified by Raymond Williams. However, the minority view of Lawrence's social philosophy, clearly articulated by Eugene Goodheart, places it in the tradition of violent tablet-breakers and aligns him with such figures as Blake, Nietzsche, Rilke and Freud. Neither placing is entirely satisfactory for either writer, since Blake belongs to both traditions, and Lawrence's knowledge of Blake's well-known lines about the "dark satanic mills," which he would have sung at school, lies behind his whole critique of industrialisation, yet at least Goodheart's placing does not make the mistake of seeing Lawrence as someone dedicated to justice and moderate social reform. As Goodheart suggests, Lawrence habitually imagines a life beyond society. In *The Rainbow* and *Women in Love*, the novelist compares the inauthentic social self with the authentic personal self and sees the one as the enemy of the other. "The conflict between the Lawrentian hero and the world is often resolved by abolishing the world."[23] His world view is based on a passionate quarrel with society; and, in this respect, he is at one with the Blake of the Prophetic Books. Both recognise the dualism supposed by life in society, both believe that the regeneration of man cannot take place without throwing off all social bonds and yet both cherish a millenarian faith in the creation of a new Jerusalem. For Blake it comes from the intercession of Jesus, who appears before Albion as the good shepherd at the conclusion of *Jerusalem* to inaugurate a splendid awakening:

> Awake! Awake, Jerusalem! O lovely Emanation of Albion,
> Awake and overspread all nations as in ancient time—
> For lo! the night of death is past and the eternal day
> Appears upon our hills! Awake, Jerusalem, and come away!

For Lawrence it comes, if it comes at all, from a return to the feudal, organic society where the bond between man and nature had not been sundered by the blind forces of mechanism, the organic society celebrated in the opening pages of *The Rainbow*. "The machine principle is equated with disintegration," as Colin Clarke has pointed out; on the other hand, "disintegration is part of the organic cycle," and Lawrence's essay on Poe makes it clear that he accepts the need for some kind of radical disintegration before achieving a higher harmony: "old things will die and disintegrate ... before anything else can come to pass."[24]

A belief in the liberation of man and society through love and the wisdom of the body is common to both writers but it takes rather different forms in each. In Blake we do not find that emphasis on the preservation of separateness in love that is a major theme in Lawrence's novels, especially *Women in Love*. For the Romantic poet the polarities of maleness and femaleness are not only part of a larger scheme of contraries but are transcended by love and imagination. Such an androgynous ideal is utterly remote from Lawrence's celebration of a necessary distinction between the sexes and the preservation of a star equilibrium, but it is difficult to believe that the apocalyptic fervour with which Lawrence writes about the redeeming power of sexual love does not owe much to Blake even though his debt to Freud is more obvious, especially in *Fantasia of the Unconscious* where he draws sharp distinctions between the sexes and sexual roles, asserting that "every bit, every cell in a boy is male, every cell is female in a woman, and must remain so," and that "women live for ever by feeling, and men live for ever from an inherent sense of purpose."[25] However, just as Blake inverts Christian values in *The Marriage of Heaven and Hell* so Lawrence inverts the Freudian idea of the unconscious existing in a state of repression and offers an apocalyptic vision of the creative role of the unconscious if there were no repression.[26] The unconscious is not, as in Freud, the enemy of order and civilisation but the potential creator of a new form of civilisation.

Lawrence's faith in blood knowledge and "the mystery of the penis" is a much more localised vindication of sensual knowledge than we find in Blake. Moreover, it often assumes a distinctly antireligious form, as it does in *The First Lady Chatterley*. "It is the penis alone which saves men from utterly destroying the world, and the phallus alone is the symbol of our unison in the blood. The cross, as the symbol of the murdered phallus, is an evil symbol and carries evil wherever it goes."[27] It is passages such as this that make it impossible to accept Graham Hough's emphasis on Christian love in Lawrence. The fact that Lawrence sees in Jesus "the ego triumphant, the spuriousness of the ego trying to seize the crown that belongs only to the consummation" casts further doubt on Hough's thesis.[28]

The extent to which the whole Romantic tradition was antirational and anti-scientific has been endlessly debated, but as the result of modern scholarship it is now clear that Wordsworth's idea of the Imagination was synonymous with a higher form of reason, that what Coleridge and Blake were opposed to was a limited empiricism, not reason, and that several of the Romantic poets, including Coleridge and Shelley, were deeply and practically interested in the scientific theories of their day. It is also clear that the central dynamic of their poetry was the tension between contrary powers, particularly the tension between feeling and intellect. All Lawrence's writing arises from a similar dynamic. But as far as attitudes to reason and science are concerned important qualifications need to be made. In *The Politics of Vision*, Mark Schorer points out that Blake's anti-rationalism never led him to the extremes of anti-intellectualism, unenlightened naturalism and total mysticism sometimes found in Lawrence;[29] Blake's serious critique of science was also very different from the reaction of Yeats and Lawrence, which was personal and negative. What all this amounts to perhaps is that Blake's world view is fundamentally more comprehensive and systematic.

Two very general qualities in Lawrence suggest that he owes much to Blake. These are the peculiar intensity of his writing and his revolutionary stance. The intensity springs from Lawrence's instinctive response to the beauty and wonder of the world and his creation of new rhythms and images to express this response. It does not spring in either writer from compression and fine economy of phrase, since both often employ an apparently clumsy and repetitive rhetoric, yet it is a deeply felt rhetoric that achieves a miraculous incandescence at climactic moments, as in Blake's celebration of the defeat of Mystery and the liberation of the "slave grinding at the mill" in the ninth night of *Vala, or the Four Zoas*, or in Lawrence's description of the moon "exploding" in the water in chapter 19 of *Women in Love*. "The furthest waves of light, fleeing out, seemed to be clamouring against the shore for escape, the waves of darkness came in heavily, running under towards the centre. But at the centre, the heart of all, was still a vivid, incandescent quivering of a white moon not quite destroyed, a white body of fire writhing and striving and not even now broken upon, not yet violated." Phrases from Lawrence's Foreword to *Women in Love* help to explain how it is that repetition and intensity can not only coexist but the one produce the other. The "continually slightly modified repetition" expresses a "pulsing, frictional to-and-fro which works up to culmination"; and the same movement and effect are found in the greatest passages in Blake's Prophetic Books.[30]

The revolutionary stance adopted by both writers is not in any limited sense a matter of political persuasion or commitment. It is an expression of an attitude to the past and the future, to all rigid and outmoded forms of human activity and to the new creative forces waiting to be released. In the introductory address to *Jerusalem*, Blake asserts that "poetry fettered, fetters the human race" and explains why he needed to create a "variety in every line both of cadences & number of syllables." He knew that he must reject the literary forms of the past in order to enact the forces of the future. In the Preface to *Milton*, he specifically addresses the "young men of the new age," calling on them to build the new Jerusalem "in England's green and pleasant land." "Rouse up, O young men of the new age! Set your foreheads against ignorant hirelings! For we have hirelings in the camp, the court and the university, who would if they could depress mental and prolong corporeal war." Although Lawrence's attitude towards purely mental struggle was distinctly sceptical, he casts himself in the same role as Blake as the destroyer of old forms and the inaugurator of new. He, too, speaks to the young men of the new age and knows that such speech needs fresh accents and rhythms related to his revolutionary stance towards past and future. The discussion of free verse in the Preface to his *New Poems* (1950) makes this clear:

> All we can say is that free verse does *not* have the same nature as restricted verse. It is not of the nature of reminiscence. It is not the past which we treasure in its perfection between our hands. Neither is it the crystal of the perfect future, into which we gaze. Its tide is neither the full, yearning flow of aspiration, nor the sweet, poignant ebb of remembrance and regret. The past and the future are the two great bournes of human emotion, the two great homes of the human days, the two eternities. They are both conclusive, final.[31]

The impulse to create a new kind of novel sprang from a similar recognition that old forms distorted reality and prevented the writer from creating a sense of the living moment in all its wholeness. Much has been written about Lawrence's rejection of the stable ego as a basis for characterisation, but no one has pointed out the close similarity between Lawrence's and Blake's cosmic psychodramas, presumably because the one is in prose and the other in verse. In Blake's Prophetic Books as in Lawrence's later fiction character and plot are of minimal significance; they exist only to embody the psychic forces that struggle to achieve full consciousness, harmony and fulfilment. Blake's twofold psychological division into Spectre and Emanation, the one masculine and the other feminine, and the dramatic engagement between these polar opposites, provided Lawrence with a model for charting deep-seated irrational conflicts in human nature. The extreme fluidity of movement, the ease with which characters temporarily merge and take on the gestures and behaviour of their opposites, the abandonment of rational causation, the moral ambiguity, are features common to the imaginative worlds of both writers. And in both, nature is not a scenic background against which the human action is played out but an intrinsic part of the creative flux.

Ultimately the advantage of talking about Lawrence as writing within the Blake tradition is that it enables one to point to something large and more indefinable than local parallels or occasional affinities. The imaginative universes we inhabit as we read these two writers of genius have remarkable general similarities. There is the same combination of innocent eye and apocalyptic fervour, the same sense of being involved in a life and death struggle with mysterious forces within oneself and in the external world, the same vision of the polarities of existence that transcends the distinctions between good and evil, natural and supernatural, male and female; finally, the same firm grounding of the mystical and mythopoeic in the concrete world of physical sensation.

CHAPTER TWO

# Lawrence and Carlyle

## PAUL DELANY

When considering D. H. Lawrence's use of tradition, we should recognize that he dedicated his career to two parallel and mutually inconsistent projects. One was a cult of absolute spontaneity and openness to the natural world—the writer as medium. In this role, Lawrence accepted limits to rendering experience that were set by the English language, but not those derived from the existing body of literature; for what mattered was the deep source of emotion, which existed independently of any previous attempts to describe it. The writer's task, therefore, was to be *original* in the most literal sense of the word. But Lawrence's other project was quite different: to be not so much a writer as a *re*-writer who exposed the failures of his predecessors to pluck out the heart of life's mystery. This compulsive re-writing is seen at its most extreme in his defacement of Bertrand Russell's lecture notes on social reconstruction.[1] It appears elsewhere in Lawrence's prolonged struggle with the *oeuvre* of Thomas Hardy, or in *The Rainbow*'s implicit critique of earlier heroines like Jane Eyre or Madame Bovary. Most important, surely, is Lawrence's re-writing not just of other authors' works but also of his own. Unlike the literary artisans who painstakingly filed and polished their works into shape, Lawrence would discard one draft after another, each time making a completely fresh start on the book. To rationalize this practice he would speak of the work being newly conceived or inspired; but the shadow of the previous attempt necessarily falls on the blank sheet that lies ready to receive the current one. And somewhere behind *that* shadow are the shadows of those other writers who have attempted the same theme.

It is in this sense that we may understand Lawrence's famous remark to Edward Garnett: "We have to hate our immediate predecessors, to get free from their authority." But the word *immediate* marks an important qualification to the rule. Lawrence had sent Garnett three plays he had written at Lake Garda, and he was arguing that the time had come for a reaction against the popular contemporary dramatists such as Shaw, Galsworthy, Ibsen and Strindberg. "You are about the only man," he told Garnett, "who is willing to let a new generation come in. It will seem a bit rough to me, when I am 45, and must see myself and my tradition supplanted."[2]

These comments suggest that Lawrence saw the major Victorians as much less intrusive rivals than the established writers of his own era. To resist his contemporaries, while finding sustenance among remoter ancestors, might effect what the Russian Formalists called "The Knight's Move"; the choice of such an indirect strategy could make Lawrence free of the conventional lines of succession and generational rivalry. To his immediate forerunners he was necessarily more hostile; some only needed to be cut down to size with a modicum of contempt, while others (such as Henry James) were dealt out a more distanced and respectful criticism. The most prominent of them, Thomas Hardy, was allotted a whole book. Carlyle, however, did not have to be grappled with openly. His voice was so idiosyncratic and stentorian that it would have been futile either to mimic him, or to try and out-shout him; yet his very uniqueness of style made it easier for Lawrence to quietly cultivate their underlying affinities.[3]

We know from Jessie Chambers' testimony that Lawrence went through a phase, around the age of twenty, when he read widely in Carlyle and was deeply impressed by him.[4] This admiration is to be expected, given their common ground in British puritanism and German idealist philosophy. From this heritage came their uncertain attitudes towards material experience: is it merely base, or does it mediate between the individual mind and the world of the spirit? Carlyle, of course, inclined more to the former position than Lawrence did; and when he did admit the worth of the material he excluded what was for Lawrence its most redemptive mode—the erotic.

*Sartor Resartus* proposes, at different times, what might be called a "hard" and a "soft" idealism. The former is rigorously Hegelian. "All visible things," proclaims Carlyle, "are emblems; what thou seest is not there on its own account; strictly taken, is not there at all: Matter exists only spiritually, and to represent some Idea, and body it forth."[5] In this model of the world there are only two radically opposed elements, Matter and Spirit. Elsewhere, however, Carlyle introduces a mediator between them: flesh. Whatever is merely excremental, a lifeless enemy of the spirit, must be cast off; but beneath it lies something of more substantial worth. "Round his mysterious ME, there lies, under all those wool-rags, a Garment of Flesh (or of Senses), contextured in the Loom of Heaven" (*Sartor*, p. 65). In *Heroes and Hero-Worship* Carlyle borrows from Novalis an even more exalted judgement of the flesh: "There is but one temple in the Universe, and that is the Body of Man . . . We touch Heaven when we lay our hand on a human body!"[6] From this judgement, however, he does not go on to the same conclusion as Lawrence. The highest mode of communion between bodies is not sexual intercourse, but rather Hero-worship: "heartfelt prostrate admiration, submission, burning, boundless, for a noblest godlike Form of Man" (*Heroes*, p. 18).

Carlylean hero-worship is a kind of eroticism, and one that largely replaces the "lower," more domestic varieties—one need not labour the contrast between the Lawrencean ideal of marriage and the unhappy, unconsummated union between Thomas and Jane Carlyle. The bond between hero and follower is implicitly homoerotic, though in so sublimated a form that immediate sensuous contact is out of the question; one cannot imagine in Carlyle anything like the wrestling match between Birkin and Gerald in *Women in Love*. Carlyle excludes, also, eroticism as a means of fostering an ideal democracy. There is a long tradition in which desire is anarchic, popular, and gives the only pleasure that is equally accessible to all; such themes, whereby sex becomes subversive of social hierarchies, are expounded by visionaries like Blake, Whitman, and Lawrence himself. Carlyle, however, glorifies the hero's body at the expense of everyone else's, and relegates *them* to a lower, more crudely material plane of being. Indeed, the hero's body becomes a noble and transcendental symbol rather than warm flesh; the greatest hero of all, for Carlyle, is Christ—by definition, the most spiritual of all bodies that have lived. Other heroes may approach Christ by subduing their baser appetites, or by charismatically drawing men on to higher realms of thought and belief. The Carlylean concept of the hero is epitomized in Hegel's cry on first seeing Napoleon: "I have seen the World Spirit, mounted upon a white horse."

Carlyle's ideals of leadership grow naturally from his early indoctrination in Scottish Calvinism, despite his turn away from organized religion in adulthood. Nearly half the protagonists of *Heroes and Hero-worship* are religious figures: Odin, Mahomet, Luther, Knox, Cromwell. "Is not every true Reformer," he demands rhetorically, "by the nature of him, a *Priest* first of all?" (*Heroes*, p. 188). The rule of the Carlylean hero is implicitly justified by the puritan doctrine of the elect, which sanctions his imposition of order on the unregenerate masses. Even after the Restoration of 1660, Scottish puritanism had remained capable of dictating to the whole community in matters of faith and morals. Lawrence's English Congregationalism, on the other hand, had to be content with a narrower domain, one consonant with the more pluralistic society around it. Carlyle's hero is typically a zealot; he must be a "son of Order," for "is not all work of man in this world a *making of Order?*" (*Heroes*, p. 328). Lawrence's hero will probably bring less order, rather than more—like Attila, for example, who smashes old cities in order to clear the way for new ones to arise.[7]

Lawrence's own phase of hero-worship lasted about ten years, beginning with his anti-democratic letters to Bertrand Russell in the summer of 1915; representative works of this time are "Education of the People," *Movements in European History*, *Aaron's Rod*, *Kangaroo* and *The Plumed Serpent*. His authoritarianism was largely a reaction against England's involvement in the First World War. To him, the war showed that democracy had little to do with wise self-government; rather, it allowed the masses to indulge in a passion for hatred and destruction. Nonetheless, Lawrence remained contemptuous of the European absolute rulers of his time—whether the Kaiser, the Czar or Mussolini. His so-called "leadership novels" present a different kind of hero: one whose potency is as much sensuous as political. The Australian leader, Kangaroo, pleads on his deathbed for a recognition of "the faithful, fearless love of man for man"; such a man, if he ever came to power, would be no Carlylean ascetic embodying the spirit of history. Rather, he would inaugurate an era of sensual unanimity between ruler and ruled.

In the terminology proposed by Harold Bloom, Lawrence's development of the Carlylean hero-cult would fall into the class of *Tessera*, "completion and antithesis," where "the precursor is regarded as an over idealizer."[8] Lawrence re-introduces the Carlylean hero to the world of the senses, and he does not shrink from the domestic or erotic humiliations that a hero may encounter there.

Furthermore, Lawrence came to recognize that when a hero is brought down to earth he may be well advised to stay there, renouncing his claim to be a superman. Kate Leslie, in *The Plumed Serpent*, intermittently denies the heroic pretensions of her husband Don Cipriano, though the conflict is left unresolved at the end of the novel. In *The Escaped Cock*, the hero himself elects to abdicate his role of redeemer to mankind and withdraw into a life of sensuous anonymity. Mellors' utter contempt for all social hierarchies, in *Lady Chatterley's Lover*, completes Lawrence's renunciation of the will to power (his disillusionment can be measured by the progressive depoliticization of Mellors in the three versions of the novel). At the end, heroism is to be exercised solely in the confrontation with sexual shame and fear, and to be confirmed solely through complete sexual consummation.

The crucial difficulty with the heroic ideal is how to generalize it. Carlyle's solution was to advocate *work* as the means of demotic heroism—a secular vocation of which all men are capable, and to which all are bound. The merely natural life disgusts him, since it allows the fallen world to remain fallen, without any redemptive order or discipline; in "The Nigger Question," for example, he harps obsessively on the black man living in cheerful idleness with his face in a pumpkin. What "The Everlasting Yea" means, in practice, is to "Produce! Produce! . . . Whatsoever thy hand findeth to do, do it with thy whole might" (*Sartor*, p. 197). These particular verses in the Carlylean gospel are formally rejected by Lawrence, in *Study of Thomas Hardy*:

> Oh, my God, work is the great body of life, and sleep and amusement like two wings, bent only to carry it along. Is this, then, all?
> And Carlyle gets up and says, It is all, and mankind goes on in grim, serious approval, more than acquiescent, approving, thinking itself religiously right.
> But let us pull the tail out of the mouth of this serpent. Eternity is not a process of eternal self-inglutination. . . .
> Work is, simply, the activity necessary for the production of a sufficient supply of food and shelter: nothing more holy than that. It is the producing of the means of self-preservation. Therefore it is obvious that it is not the be-all and the end-all of existence. We work to provide means of subsistence, and when we have made provision, we proceed to live.[9]

The social aim of Carlyle's "Gospel of Work" is the creation of a unanimous productive will, so that Britain can advance towards its national destiny—already defined in *Chartism* as "the grand Industrial task of conquering some half or more of this Terraqueous Planet for the use of man."[10] First on the agenda is to "dethrone that Brute-god Mammon, and put a Spirit-god in his place!";[11] once that is achieved, progress may take its natural—or unnatural—course. When Carlyle derided the "gross, steam engine Utilitarianism" of Bentham (*Heroes*, p. 299), he was not rejecting the steam engine as such. "The Life-tree Igdrasil," he observes, "in all its new developments, is the selfsame world-old Life-tree. . . . A 'Splendour of God,' in one form or other, will have to unfold itself from the heart of these our Industrial Ages too; or they will never get themselves 'organised. . . . An actual new Sovereignty, Industrial Aristocracy, real not imaginary Aristocracy, is indispensable and indubitable for us" (*Past and Present*, pp. 334–335).

It was Carlyle, after all, who coined a name for the new class, the "Captains of Industry"; and it is instructive to compare that chapter of *Past and Present* with *Women in Love*'s "The Industrial Magnate." For Carlyle, the evils of industrialism are only *by-products*—of the cash-nexus, *laissez-faire* and the trade cycle. The remedy for them is to be sought in the past: by inducing today's industrialists to emulate the virtues of the medieval knights:

> No Working World, any more than a Fighting World, can be led on without a noble Chivalry of Work, and laws and fixed rules which follow out of that,—far nobler than any Chivalry of Fighting was. As an anarchic multitude on mere Supply-and-demand, it is becoming inevitable that we dwindle in horrid suicidal convulsion, and self-abrasion, frightful to the imagination, into *Chactaw* Workers. With wigwam and scalps,—with palaces and thousand-pound bills; with savagery, depopulation, chaotic desolation!   (*Past and Present*, p. 365)

Unregulated capitalism thus slides down into barbarism; but if the industrialists take on their proper role of "Fighters against Chaos," all may yet be well. They must begin by admitting the spiritual into their task, instead of being soulless utilitarians. Then they should keep employment constant when trade is slow, and strive for a more equal distribution of what industry can produce. Instead of being "unregimented, anarchic," the working world would answer to the divine principle of organization.[12]

Mr Crich, of *Women in Love*, approaches the Carlylean ideal of what a capitalist should be, though his paternalism owes more to primitive Christianity than to chivalry. "He had never lost this from his heart," Lawrence observes, "that in Christ he was one with his workmen."[13] But opposition within his own family, and from outside, reduces Mr Crich to a beaten man long before he dies. His wife despises him for his cringing charity, and his workers for his failure to assert authority over them. Because he refuses to modernize, the family enterprise is on the verge of collapse when Gerald takes it over. Lawrence's account of Gerald's regime exposes the dynamics of modern capitalism with a penetration and grasp of detail that go far beyond Carlyle, who so often substitutes bombast for analysis. Gerald turns himself into "the God of the machine"; discarding his father's humanitarianism, he pursues a vision of "the pure instrumentality of mankind." Instead of a nominal equality with their masters—which neither side had really believed in—the miners are now given "participation in a great and perfect system that subjected life to pure mathematical principles . . . the substitution of the mechanical principle for the organic" (pp. 250, 260). And the mines thrive as never before.

So far, Lawrence's critique of modern industry is congruent with Carlyle's, though better grounded in the actual workings of a coal-mining society. It is in portraying the *psychology* of the industrialist that he breaks new ground. Gerald is shown to be possessed by a semi-religious craving for order—"translating the mystic word harmony into the practical word organization" (p. 256). But within this principle of order is a kernel of nihilism, revealed in Gerald's hankering after the primitive and his reduction of women to objects of sensation. His emotional degeneration and eventual suicide are shown to be intimately linked to his success in the role of industrialist. The contrast with Carlyle is stark. Equating anarchic capitalism with savagery, Carlyle envisioned a regimented capitalism that alone could save Britain from chaos. Lawrence claimed that the higher the degree of organization, the greater the nihilism and dissolution at the core.

From their differences over the future of industrialism, we may gain a perspective on the issue of whether Carlyle and Lawrence can be considered precursors of fascism and Nazism. I would argue that Carlyle's political tracts, especially the *Latter-day Pamphlets* and *Shoot-*

*ing Niagara: and After?*, present a much closer anticipation of fascism than any theory that may be extracted from Lawrence's writings. In his "leadership phase" Lawrence held three main beliefs in common with fascism: scorn for representative democracy, support for a charismatic leader who rules with the aid of a caste of pledged followers, and the adumbration of a national myth rooted in primitive symbolism. But Lawrence's fascism, if it can even be called that, is a head severed from limbs and trunk; for it does not provide the executive means for its own implementation. Fascism as a functional political doctrine is based on the total mobilization of the state for definite ends: imperialism, racial hegemony of a favoured group, rapid development of industry and of the armed forces. All of these ends, in fact, were part of Carlyle's agenda for Victorian Britain. The one aspect of fascism lacking in Carlyle—though it is no small lack—is that peculiarly twentieth-century invention, the police state.

If one seeks an explanation of why Lawrence should so diverge from Carlyle politically, despite the considerable similarity of temperament between the two men, the simplest answer would be that Lawrence had learned from history, and from his compulsive travels. He had seen the countryside round Eastwood despoiled by industry, seen the cultural annihilation of primitive peoples, lived with the daily impact of the Defence of the Realm regulations and the regime of Mussolini. Harshest lesson of all, probably, was his subjection to the demands of conscription and his expulsion from his home in Cornwall by the army in 1917. Though he once said that what man needed from life was "magic, mystery, and authority," the authorities that he actually encountered almost always seemed to him oppressive, soulless and illegitimate.

The fundamental urge in both Lawrence and Carlyle is nostalgia for the old hierarchical, organic or "face-to-face" society; however, Carlyle envisions an organic society *with* industrialism, Lawrence an organic society *without* it. One choice gives the basic recipe for fascism, whereas the other leads to something more like the "green parties" of Western Europe today, dedicated to ecological preservation and the defense of regional interests. Lawrence's poem "Future States" suggests his affinity with such movements:

> Once men touch one another, then the modern industrial form of
>     machine civilisation will melt away
> and universalism and cosmopolitanism will cease;

the great movement of centralising into oneness will stop
and there will be a vivid recoil into separateness;
many vivid small states, like a kaleidoscope, all colours
and all the differences given expression.

The issues of centralization and imperialism display the differences between Carlyle and Lawrence on a world-wide stage. Carlyle began his intellectual career in provincial isolation, but was gradually drawn to London, the capital of culture and politics. At one point when his career refused to thrive in the early 1830s he toyed with the idea of becoming a backwoodsman in America; but after the success of *The French Revolution* he became settled to the verge of inertia. He lived in the same London house for almost fifty years, travelled reluctantly and spent most of his waking hours in a soundproof room of his own design (long before Proust had thought of such a refuge). Lawrence, who could easily write in a crowded room or sitting under a tree, had no inclination to rest and gather moss. His wanderlust was partly driven by the search for a healthful climate, but more basic was his sense of the exhaustion of Western culture and its need to be revitalized, from sources either outside or below the established way of life he had known. He believed that the age-long European ascendancy was nearing its end: "our spirit and our manhood begin to weaken, our idea and our ideal begin to peter out."[14]

For Lawrence, then, a Europe that had lost faith in itself could no longer claim the right to extend its way of life into new territory. His quarrel with nineteenth-century imperialism is expressed by Don Ramón in *The Plumed Serpent*:

> The leaves of one great tree can't hang on the boughs of another great tree. The races of the earth are like trees, in the end they neither mix nor mingle.... Only from the flowers there is commingling. And the flowers of every race are the natural aristocrats of that race.... Only the Natural Aristocrats can rise above their nation; and even then they do not rise beyond their race. Only the Natural Aristocrats of the World can be international, or cosmopolitan, or cosmic. It has always been so.[15]

The breakdown of traditional cultures in the modern era, and the corresponding growth of a unitary world system, has been taking place under the hegemony of the Western industrial nations; but even if it had come about by the free association of equals Lawrence still would have been against it. Relations between countries or races are for him analogous to those between men and women: they are most fruitful when each partner recognizes the irreconcilable differences between them, and respects the other's separateness. Mutual receptiveness must have a place for mutual difference; if not, there will ensue either a demonic clash of wills or a mechanical grinding down of the weaker party by the stronger. A late review by Lawrence sums up his disillusionment with Western colonialism, and with the so-called heroes who had brought it to the New World:

> Men of action are usually deadly failures in the long run. Their precious energy makes them uproot the tree of life, and leave it to wither, and their stupidity makes them proud of it. Even in [Pedro de] Valdivia, and he seems to have been as human as any Conquistador, the stone blindness to any mystery or meaning in the Indians themselves, the utter unawareness of the fact that they might have a point of view, the abject insensitiveness to the strange, eerie atmosphere of that America he was proceeding to exploit and to ruin, puts him at a certain dull level of intelligence which we find rather nauseous. The world has suffered so cruelly from these automatic men of action. (*Phoenix*, p. 358)

The worst that might be said of Lawrence's attitude to non-Western societies is that he had the mentality of a highly sensitive and intelligent tourist—a role that must itself be tainted with colonialism, albeit subtly and indirectly. He went to foreign countries as he went to women: in search of emotional nourishment. To get it, he would at times see those around him in whatever light suited his own needs. Still, Lawrence sought to preserve the greatest possible diversity of ways of life; whereas Carlyle dreamed of imposing on the world a Prussian uniformity. Consistently Carlyle extols the domination of the weak by the strong, whether it be in his support of Eyre, the Hanging Governor of Jamaica, or in his rhapsody on the virtues of drill:

> I always fancy there might much be done in the way of military Drill withal. Beyond all other schooling, and as supplement or even as succedaneum for all other, one often wishes the entire Population could be thoroughly drilled; into cooperative movement, into individual behaviour, correct, precise, and at once habitual and orderly as mathematics, in all or in very many

points,—and ultimately in the point of actual *Military Service*, should such be required of it![16]

To conclude, some thoughts on the question of style. Carlyle's philosophy, which defines human knowledge as partial, intermittent and epiphanic, anticipates our modern preoccupation with the crisis of representation. "Everywhere do the Shows of things oppress [Teufelsdrockh]," he writes in *Sartor*, "withstand him, threaten him with fearfullest destruction: only by victoriously penetrating into Things themselves can he find peace and a stronghold" (p. 206). The continuing metaphor here is one of taking off clothes in order to reveal the essential body of truth beneath. Carlyle is not unaware that perhaps the most obstructive of these garments is the medium of language itself; from this stems his well-known obsession with the idea that the deepest truths lie buried in silence.[17] Nonetheless, his own prose is relentlessly *dense*, continually drawing attention to itself rather than what it claims to represent. Works that extol the supremacy of the spirit are written in a thickly material prose, that bears everywhere the signs of a fetishism of the word.

Carlyle's defense of his style was that it could not be artificial because it had been inherited. It originated, he told Froude, "in the old farmhouse at Annandale. The humour of it came from his mother. The form was his father's common mode of speech, and had been adopted by himself for its brevity and emphasis. He was aware of its singularity and feared that it might be mistaken for affectation, but it was a natural growth."[18] Because it was an organic means of expression, he argued, it could not be accused of interposing a veil between the reader and the natural world: "people seem to think a style can be put off or put on not like a *skin* but like a coat! Now I refer it to Sterling himself (enemy as he is), whether a skin be not verily the product and close kinsfellow of all that lies under it; exact type of the nature of the beast: *not* to be plucked off without flaying and death?" (Froude, p. 340). What this image suggests, however, is that style represents its author, rather than the external world; at best, that any world represented must be a peculiarly Carlylean one. No doubt we all see our own worlds; but the one Carlyle sees is more than usually introspective. His prose is quite devoid of specific observation or striking visual imagery; it is above all *portentous*, continually evoking mysteries that are too deep to be vulgarly broadcast:

> He who takes not counsel of the Unseen and Silent, from him will never come real visibility and speech. Thou must descend to the *Mothers*, to the *Manes*, and Hercules-like long suffer and labour there, wouldst thou emerge with victory into the sunlight. . . . You look fixedly into Madness, and *her* undiscovered, boundless, bottomless Night-empire; that you may extort new Wisdom out of it, as an Eurydice from Tartarus. . . . All Works, each in their degree, are a making of Madness sane. (*Past and Present*, pp. 276–277)

Passages like this deploy a self-absorbed rhetoric that has little concern to render experience communicable. They are designed, rather, to support Carlyle's pretensions to high authority. His world-view, we are asked to believe, has been forged in a harrowing, but ultimately unnameable ordeal of consciousness.

There would be little point here in illustrating, by way of contrast, Lawrence's mastery of descriptive prose. Rather, let us examine him when he is closest to Carlyle's own ground, speaking of one of his own nervous crises early in the Great War:

> I am struggling in the dark—very deep in the dark—and cut off from everybody and everything. . . . Sometimes I am afraid of the terrible things that are real, in the darkness, and of the entire unreality of these things I see. It becomes like a madness at last, to know one is all the time walking in a pale assembly of an unreal world—this house, the furniture, the sky and the earth—whilst oneself is all the while a piece of darkness pulsating in shocks, and the shocks and the darkness are real.[19]

It is evident, I think, that Lawrence is here *evoking* the underworld, rather than just *invoking* it as Carlyle does. He is attempting, that is, to convey some immediate emotional and physical impression of the descent into madness, while still remaining coherent. The difficulties of doing so are obvious, and many readers have felt unsatisfied by Lawrence's rhapsodic accounts of experiences—whether metaphysical or sexual ones—that perhaps are ultimately resistant to being described. Nonetheless, his distinction between *statement* and *creation* is an appropriate one to apply to the two passages just quoted. When comparing them, one sees the force of Leavis's objection to coupling Lawrence with Carlyle—essentially on the grounds that one man was an artist, and the other was not.[20]

What, finally, are we to make of Lawrence's remark to Blanche Jennings in 1908; that two years earlier he had been "suffering acutely from Carlyliophobia, which you will understand if that rabid philosopher has ever bitten you" (*Letters*, I. 49). Unfortunately, few of Lawrence's letters have survived from that period, when he was beginning his studies at Nottingham University College. But there may be a clue in some advice he gave to Louie Burrows about her writing, in September 1906: "I like above all things your enthusiasm, and your delightful fresh, youthful feeling. Don't be didactic; try and make things reveal their mysteries to you, then tell them over simply and swiftly, without exaggerating as I do" (*Letters*, I. 30). One can see here a hint of Lawrence's wariness against the intrusion of Carlylean tendencies into his own prose.[21] To be thus "bitten" by Carlyle would mean to become his instrument and inferior, driven compulsively by the virus of his pessimism, isolation and high transcendentalism. The kinship that Lawrence felt with Carlyle made him only the more dangerous as a spiritual mentor and interpreter of the world's mysteries.

When, therefore, Bloom ranks Lawrence among the "great deniers of influence" (*Anxiety*, p. 56), one should note that this applies to *literary* influence only. Lawrence resisted and mistrusted his great literary predecessors because they threatened to make him see the natural world through their eyes rather than his own. If this happened, his vision would be obscured by an alien veil of language; and the thickest such veil would be the clotted and fetishised style of writers like Carlyle. Lawrence's literary project assumed that it was possible to recover an Edenic language, able to lie passive and transparent to the splendours of natural forces. Influence could then be raised to a far higher plane than the mere bartering of literary shreds and patches; it would be transformed from inhibition to inspiration, as foretold by the grand Romantic myth of the Aeolian harp:

> Not I, not I, but the wind that blows through me!
> A fine wind is blowing the new direction of Time.
> If only I let it bear me, carry me, if only it carry me!
> If only I am sensitive, subtle, oh, delicate, a winged gift!
> If only, most lovely of all, I yield myself and am borrowed
> By the fine, fine wind that takes its course through the chaos of the world

Like a fine, an exquisite chisel, a wedge-blade inserted;
If only I am keen and hard like the sheer tip of a wedge
Driven by invisible blows,
The rock will split, we shall come at the wonder, we shall find the Hesperides.[22]

CHAPTER THREE

# Lawrence and Ruskin: The Sage as Word-Painter

## GEORGE P. LANDOW

Three decades ago Richard Aldington recognized that Lawrence was "strangely akin" to John Ruskin, the great Victorian critic of art and society, "both in the character of his mind and in his social views—a certain affinity and an unadmitted literary influence."[1] Keith Alldritt, who points out that "Lawrence grew to maturity at a time when Ruskin was still regarded as a major writer," claims that "though his attitude to Ruskin was always critical, it was never altogether dismissive. . . . Ruskinism . . . was more than a mere set of ideas to Lawrence; it was rather a particular range of emotional reverberation which he had known both in himself and in others."[2] Although a few critics and biographers have thus pointed to Ruskin's major influence upon D. H. Lawrence, most have failed to build upon their recognitions. Most writers on Lawrence, it is true, do remark that Ruskin influenced his hatred of industrialism,[3] and Keith Sagar, one of the few to perceive a Ruskinian presence, has pointed out that his notion of the snake as "a divine hieroglyph of the demoniac power of the earth—of the entire earthly Nature" anticipates Lawrence's discussion of the serpent's mythic status in *Etruscan Places* and other works.[4] Such recognitions of Ruskin's influence, however, have been comparatively rare, and students of Lawrence have generally failed to perceive the novelist's complex relation to his predecessor.

In fact, certain areas of Lawrence criticism which one might expect to mention Ruskin frequently are marked, instead, by an almost complete failure to do so. For example, David J. Gordon's useful *D. H. Lawrence as a Literary Critic* concerns an aspect of Lawrence's writings which obviously demands relating to Ruskin, if only

35

to point out either that Lawrence rejects his predecessor's ideas or that he formulates his own in direct reaction to them. Gordon thus points out that "the flexible, freewheeling form of critical essay which Lawrence developed for himself enabled him to pass naturally beyond a concern for art proper and to emphasize its relation to the civilization of which it is a vital expression."[5] In fact, all the elements Gordon credits Lawrence with inventing characterize the writings of the great Victorian critic of art and society: his freewheeling critical discussion, his movement in such criticism from art to the civilization within which it took form, and the idea that art is the best and most important expression of the society which produced it—so that to improve art one has, first, to change society itself.

Indeed, as Arnold Hauser has remarked, Ruskin

> was indubitably the first to interpret the decline of art and taste as the sign of a general cultural crisis, and to express the basic, and even today not sufficiently appreciated, principle that the conditions under which men live must first be changed, if their sense of beauty and their comprehension of art are to be awakened.... He was, finally, the first to proclaim the gospel that art is not the privilege of artists, connoisseurs and the educated classes, but is part of every man's inheritance and estate.... Ruskin attributed the decay of art to the fact that the modern factory, with its mechanical mode of production and division of labour, prevents a genuine relationship between the worker and his work, that is to say, that it crushes out the spiritual element and estranges the producer from the product of his hands.[6]

Similarly, Gordon's clear description of Lawrence's characteristic argumentative method, which employs shifting terminologies,[7] again well defines both a quality of mind and a manner of proceeding which derives from Ruskin, just as Lawrence's conceptions of analogical literary structure would also in part seem to do, for such structural principles inform *Modern Painters* and *Praeterita*, Ruskin's brilliantly allusive autobiography.[8] From Ruskin Lawrence also seems to have derived major portions of his conceptions of symbolism, particularly his emphasis on the intrinsic relation of symbol and myth.[9] Even Lawrence's basic opposition to asceticism and ideal art—a point at which one might expect to find him opposed by Ruskin—agrees completely with him.[10]

At the same time that one argues for a major Ruskinian influence upon Lawrence, one must admit that some cases may represent confluence rather than influence. For example, as many writers on Lawrence have perceived, the Bible, particularly as it was read within the English dissenting tradition, colors all of Lawrence's prose. As Alldritt has pointed out in his discussion of *The Rainbow*, Lawrence there draws upon vernacular culture for a conception of biblical epic as well as for his frequent scriptural allusion.[11] One should take such observations considerably further, since in Lawrence's references to Abraham, Moses, David and other Old Testament prefigurations of Christ and Christian doctrine he shares with Ruskin and many other Victorians a habit of secularized, often ironic, allusions not only to specific biblical texts but also to the interpretive tradition in which they were understood.[12] Thus, Lawrence places his new rainbow against traditional nonconformist readings of that natural phenomenon as a covenant-sign and type of the Saviour. One recognizes additional rich ironic reverberations when one also perceives that the chain of scriptural types throughout the novel here reaches its climax in this imagistic coda. If Lawrence learned such scriptural imagery from his religious upbringing, why need we mention Ruskin at all? Ruskin is here important because he offered Lawrence an influential example of an author reworking and reapplying such materials in writings on art, literature and society. Although Lawrence certainly learned to recognize and even think in terms of such interpretive modes in his boyhood, nonetheless Ruskin and Carlyle most likely taught him how to employ such allusions in secular prose.

Quite obviously, how one judges such relationships ultimately depends upon the critic's point of view, initial premises and purpose. If, for example, the critic engages himself to demonstrate Lawrence's superiority to his Victorian predecessors—or, to state the point more neutrally, if he wishes to emphasize what Lawrence adds to his tradition—then necessarily the critical enterprise takes the form of sharp distinctions which emphasize the new, the different, and overlooks points of contact and resemblance, be they few or many. On the other hand, the critic and cultural historian who attempts to perceive Lawrence's position within a long continuum deriving from Ruskin and beyond necessarily emphasizes precisely those points of contact the other critic, or other purpose of the same critic, de-emphasizes or even fails to perceive. Fortunately, now that Lawrence and other writers of his age have clearly won their recognition as modern masters, his readers no longer need to argue for his greatness by first cutting him off from the tradition in which he produced his work. Rather, now that we see Lawrence is a major author in his own right, we as critics and readers late in the twentieth century surely need to perceive to what extent his work arose within native traditions.

By observing how much Lawrence owes to Ruskin, one can recognize precisely where Lawrence's uniqueness, inventiveness and genius lay. Indeed, as Ruskin himself reminds us in *The Seven Lamps of Architecture* (1849), "It is no sign of deadness in present art that it borrows or imitates, but only if it borrows without paying interest, or if it imitates without choice" (8.195). Since any complete examination of the complex and often ironic relationship between Ruskin and Lawrence demands an entire volume, and a long one at that, I have chosen to devote the following pages to several related literary methods that Lawrence learned from his predecessor and then added to them, making them his own.

D. H. Lawrence clearly learned from the author of *Modern Painters* (1843–60) and *The Stones of Venice* (1851–3) various modes of visually oriented prose, just as he also learned to transform Ruskinian word-painting into symbolic or mythological set-pieces. But, as we shall observe, although many passages of Lawrence's writing, both in the travel books and fiction, clearly bear the impress of Ruskin the word-painter, many also mark his extension of them into a new way of seeing, thinking and feeling in prose.

Lawrence learned from Ruskin ways of creating powerful topographical descriptions and also the uses to which such elaborate word-painting can be put. Ruskin's famed skill at natural description, which he employs throughout *Modern Painters*, *The Stones of Venice* and his other writings, achieve their characteristic effect in large part because he infused his descriptions with a powerfully ordered energy. Ruskin's characteristic word-paintings take three basic forms, each more complex and more powerful than the last. First, he employs what we may term an additive style, one in which, like most writers of description, he cites a number of visual details one after another. The second mode, in contrast, creates a dramatized scene placed before the reader, whose attention is focused upon certain elements which move through this fictive space conjured up by language. For example, in the first volume of *Modern Painters* when Ruskin writes about rain clouds, he first explains how they form and then move in relation to the earth below, after which, like the Evangelical preacher and Romantic poet, he cites his own experience:

> I remember once, when in crossing the Tete Noire, I had turned up the valley towards Trient, I noticed a rain-cloud forming on the Glacier de Trient. With a west wind, it proceeded towards the Col de Balme, being followed by a prolonged wreath of vapour, always forming exactly at the same spot over the glacier. This long, serpent-like line of cloud went on at a great rate till it reached the valley.... There it turned sharp round, and came down this valley, at right angles to its former progress, and finally directly contrary to it, till it came down within five hundred feet of the village, where it disappeared; the line behind always advancing, and always disappearing, at the same spot. This continued for half an hour, the long line describing the curve of a horse-shoe; always coming into existence and always vanishing at exactly the same place; traversing the space between with enormous swiftness. This cloud, ten miles off, would have looked like a perfectly motionless wreath, in the form of a horse-shoe hanging over the hills. (3.395)

Ruskin thus places us before his Alpine scene, permitting us to observe the movement of a single element within it. After he has concluded his examination of the moving cloud, he moves us farther away and tells us what the same phenomenon would look like—how we would experience it—from a different point of view.

In *Twilight in Italy* Lawrence creates this kind of word-painting, which produces the effect of moving elements within a scene, when he describes his experience upon leaving the darkened, sensual interior of San Tommaso and coming out suddenly into bright day:

> Across, the heavy mountain crouched, along the side of the lake, the upper half brilliantly white, belonging to the sky, the lower half dark and grim. So, then, that is where heaven and earth are divided. From behind me, on the left, the headland swept down out of a great, pale-grey, arid height, through a rush of russet and crimson, to the olive smoke and the water of the level earth. And between, like a blade of the sky cleaving the earth asunder, went the pale-blue lake, cleaving mountain from mountain with the triumph of the sky.[13]

As this passage demonstrates, Lawrence, like Ruskin, creates his powerful descriptions by transforming description into narrative. In this instance he first implicitly places himself as viewer with the word "Across" which informs the reader where the scene takes place in relation to the perceiving eye. Then Lawrence presents the outlines of mountain form, not as static boundaries between material masses but rather as paths of movement. Thus, the mountain "crouched" before him alongside of the lake, while on his left hand the headland "swept down" from the arid heights. Since Lessing it has been a critical commonplace that the verbal arts are essentially temporal and the visual ones static. Ruskinian—and Lawrencean—word-painting uses this inevitable sequentiality of verbal art both to order and energize its attempts to create a visualizable pictorial image.[14]

Ruskin's third characteristic technique, which produces what we may anachronistically term a cinematic prose, proceeds by first establishing a center of consciousness which organizes the scene like a camera lens. Having established his narrative center or fictive eye, he proceeds to move it either through or across his described scene—that is, he either turns this camera-eye upon its axis, in effect panning across the scene, or else he changes the perceiving eye's distance to the scene, moving it closer (or into) the scene. Conversely, he moves it farther away to provide a distant view. Such literary strategies provide verbal art with a means of composing and ordering linguistic descriptions, thereby providing them with some of the elements and capacities of the visual arts. This inevitably kinetic description possesses an energy which merely additive and accumulatory forms do not. Examples of this third, or proto-cinematic, form of word-painting in Ruskin's works include his elaborate description of La Riccia (3.278–280) in the first volume of *Modern Painters* (1843), his satiric look at Claude's *Il Mulino* and the Roman scenery it purports to depict in the 1844 preface to that same volume (3.41–43) and many passages in *The Stones of Venice* (1851–53), particularly his tour of St Mark's (10. 79–90), and his aerial view of the Mediterranean Sea (10.186–187).

This kind of proto-cinematic descriptive prose appears in the opening pages of *The Rainbow*, which describe the Marsh, the home of the Brangwens. Organizing this description by first establishing a vantage point in the Ruskinian manner, Lawrence then moves this imagined, fictive eye: "looking from the garden gate down the road to the right, there, through the dark archway of the canal's square aqueduct, was a colliery spinning away in the near distance, and further, red, crude houses plastered in the valley in masses, and beyond all, the dim smoking hill of the down." Using the imagined eye's movement to create a path down which he can channel our visual imagination, Lawrence establishes the moral and philosophical meanings of the landscape within which he sets his narrative.

Lawrence also resembles Ruskin in avoiding "to be" and passive constructions, thereby creating life, movement and energy in his description. For example, in the sentence immediately after he has placed the Brangwens' home in relation to industrialization and its ravages, he first provides the reader with a meaning for the scene he is about to describe and then presents its vitality in terms of such strong verbs:

> The homestead was just on the safe side of civilisation, outside the gate. The house *stood* bare from the road, approached by a straight garden path, along which at spring the daffodils were thick in green and yellow. At the sides of the house were bushes of lilac and guelder-rose and privet, entirely *hiding* the farm buildings behind.
>
> At the back a confusion of sheds *spread* into the homeclose from out of two or three indistinct yards. The duckpond *lay* beyond the furthest wall, *littering* its white feathers on the padded earthen banks, *blowing* its stray soiled feathers into the grass and the gorse bushes below the canal embankment, which *rose* like a high rampart near at hand.   (emphasis added)

A different use of this kind of kinetic description closes this first chapter, when Lawrence, in the manner of Ruskin and Tennyson, presents a character's exterior environment expressionistically; that is, like his Victorian predecessors, he employs what Ruskin termed the Pathetic (or emotional) Fallacy, a technique which makes the setting figure forth a character's interior landscape, his mind and mood.[15] Having proposed to Lydia, Brangwen experiences his passion as "a clanging torment," for "such intimacy of embrace, and such utter foreignness of contact" torture him. He thereupon goes out into the windy night:

> Big holes were blown into the sky, the moonlight blew about. Sometimes a high moon, liquid-brilliant, scudded across a hollow space and took cover under electric, brown-iridescent cloud-

edges. Then there was a blot of cloud, and shadow. Then somewhere in the night a radiance again, like a vapour. And all the sky was teeming and tearing along, a vast disorder of flying shapes and darkness and ragged fumes of light and a great brown circling halo, then the terror of a moon running liquid-brilliant into the open for a moment, hurting the eyes before she plunged under cover of cloud again.[16]

This brilliant application of the Pathetic Fallacy as Ruskin suggested it should be employed—that is, to body forth a character's strongest emotions—receives a characteristically Laurencean intonation, since he employs it for subjects and emotions Ruskin would not himself have emphasized: physical desire and passion. Such a passage reminds us that Lawrence's natural development of Ruskinian word-painting takes the form of using such techniques learned from his Victorian master to convey precisely those experiential and imaginative truths which most concerned him—and in so doing he advanced both nonfiction and the novel into new areas.

Lawrence's own brilliant additions to the tradition of Ruskinian word-painting—the sensuous and semi-conscious feelings one experiences within a scene—appear with particular clarity in *Twilight in Italy* when he relates his experience of San Tommaso. This passage, which appears in "The Spinner and the Monks," owes a great deal to Ruskin's many presentations of prospect visions, Pisgah sights and distant views of mountains throughout his works (but particularly in *Modern Painters* and his autobiography *Praeterita*), and that section which tells of Lawrence's entrance into the church itself seems based upon Ruskin's elaborate narrative presentation of St Mark's in *The Stones of Venice*. After explaining that the "tiny chaotic back-ways" and "tortuous, tiny, deep passages of the village" baffled him, he relates how, one day, he at last managed to ascend to the church which surmounts the village. Finding a broken stairway, he runs up it, "and came out suddenly, as by a miracle, clean on the platform of my San Tommaso, in the tremendous sunshine," and he discovers himself in "another world, the world of the eagle, the world of fierce abstraction. . . . I was in the skies now." After describing his setting, first in terms of the details surrounding him and then by filling in the distant sights far below on the lake, Lawrence next ruminates upon the church he has come to investigate, after which he enters its sheltering darkness:

I went into the Church. It was very dark, and impregnated with centuries of incense. It affected me like the lair of some enormous creature. My senses were roused, they sprang awake in the hot, spiced darkness. My skin was expectant, as if it expected some contact, some embrace, as if it were aware of the contiguity of the physical world, the physical contact with the darkness and the heavy, suggestive substance of the enclosure. It was a thick, fierce darkness of the senses. But my soul shrank.

I went out again. The pavemented threshold was clear as a jewel, the marvellous clarity of sunshine that becomes blue in the height seemed to distill me into myself. (pp. 21–22)

This passage well exemplifies Lawrence's version of what Richard L. Stein has taught us to recognize as a Ruskinian "fable of perception."[17] Brilliantly as this scene departs from Ruskin's own methods by emphasizing the physical and subconscious reactions of the viewer, it nonetheless still represents Lawrence adding to rather than denying his Ruskinian heritage. In fact, Lawrence here stands in relation to Ruskin as Ruskin himself stands in relation to Sir Joshua Reynolds; each succeeding man incorporates and builds upon the ideas of his predecessor. When Reynolds attempted to win prestige for the art of painting, he found himself forced to use the only available terminology, and he therefore employed the traditional opposition between mechanical (or physical) and intellectual arts. Thus, he claimed that painting, like literature, was an intellectual art.

In contrast, Ruskin inherited the resources of Romantic tradition, and when he came to formulate his Romantic theory of the sister arts—he takes literature and painting as equivalent forms of the poetic and urges us to receive his remarks on one subject as applying to the other—added a third term, the imaginative, to the two that Reynolds had used. Therefore, he can urge that in contrast to the works produced by physical and intellectual means, poetry is produced by the higher faculty of imagination. Lawrence, who comfortably takes his place in this progression, demonstrates by his descriptive passages and narrative that he adds the unconscious and sexual drives to those faculties Ruskin had described. For Lawrence, therefore, imaginative description had to include those sensations that hover around and beneath consciousness.

Furthermore, Lawrence also builds upon Ruskin's conception of imaginative art. Several places in *Modern Painters* explain that both the novice and the painter without imagination must content themselves with a merely topographical art of visual fact. "The aid of the great inventive landscape painter," on the other hand, "must be to give the far higher and deeper truth of mental vision, rather than that of the physical facts, and to reach a representation which . . . shall yet be capable of producing on the far-away beholder's mind precisely the impression which the reality would have produced."[18] According to Ruskin, in this higher form of art, "the artist not only *places* the spectator, but . . . makes him a sharer in his own strong feelings and quick thoughts."[19] In other words, the great imaginative artist, whether he works in words or paint, grants us the privilege of momentarily seeing with his eyes and imaginative vision: we experience his phenomenological relation to the world. By including and even emphasizing elements which Ruskin had himself not included, Lawrence extends this kind of imaginative description in his own way.

In addition to thus incorporating Ruskinian phenomenological descriptions of the exterior and interior worlds into his writing, Lawrence also employs Ruskinian transformation of natural phenomena into emblems. Lawrence's emblematization of landscape set-pieces appears throughout both his travel writing and fiction. In *Sea and Sardinia*, for example, he presents the solitary figure working within the landscape as an emblem of the old full life, which he contrasts to the life of man under industrialism. He begins, as he so frequently does in such set-pieces, by presenting the scene from the vantage point of those moving through a defined space.

> Soon we begin to climb to the hills. And soon the cultivation begins to be intermittent. Extraordinary how the healthy, moor-like hills come to the sea: extraordinary how scrubby and uninhabited the great spaces of Sardinia are. It is wild, with heath and arbutus scrub and a sort of myrtle, breast-high. Sometimes one sees a few head of cattle. And then again come the greyish arable-patches, where the corn is grown. It is like Cornwall, like the Land's End region. Here and there, in the distance, are peasants working on the lonely landscape. Sometimes it is one man alone in the distance, showing so vividly in his black-and-white costume, small and far-off like a solitary magpie, and curiously

distinct. All of the strange magic of Sardinia is in this sight. Among the low, moor-like hills, away in a hollow of wide landscape one solitary figure, small but vivid black-and-white, working alone, as if eternally. There are patches and hollows of grey arable land, good for corn. Sardinia was once a great granary. (p. 71)

In one sense, Lawrence relates his experience of climbing the hills of Sardinia and encountering its people within their land much as does any picturesque traveler of the nineteenth century, for he proceeds by interspersing facts encountered with thoughts prompted by them.[20] Unlike both Ruskin's or his own pure word-painting, this passage devotes little effort to presenting visual reality. He briefly mentions an act of vision but does not present visual facts of form, color or brightness in any detail. Instead the narrating voice simply *names* the objects perceived, after which it then comments in some way upon their significance. Although Lawrence organizes the narration of his encounter with the Sardinian landscape in terms of a physical movement through it, he concentrates, not as in other places in his writing upon the experience of the visual facts, but rather upon the meaning that these facts have for him. Lawrence, in other words, here emphasizes an act of interpretation rather than one of visual perception.

Any attempt to present landscape can take three forms—the actual act of perception and the visual experience itself; the primary interpretation of experience (these patches of color are arable fields); and then the political, moral or philosophical interpretation of this second level (such fields represent man in a natural relation to an unsullied nature).[21] Lawrence, who here concerns himself with the second and third steps almost entirely, thus begins by presenting the action of the climb, then what that act of climbing first reveals —here the fact that cultivated fields become intermittent—after which the describer (or narrator) comments upon the unusual fact that the hills come so close to the sea. He next comments how "scrubby and uninhabited" are Sardinia's great spaces as if to indicate how small a role man has in this world and how little room he and his activities occupy in it. Then, after specifically mentioning the kind of vegetation which contributes to this overall impression of wildness, Lawrence mentions another visual act: "Sometimes one sees a few head of cattle." Next he compares the scene to the Land's

End region of Cornwall and this mention of native English landscape provides an analogy which makes the Sardinian landscape more understandable. Finally, he arrives at what turns out to be the intellectual center of this passage of description and the purpose to which it has been building: the appearance of solitary human beings working in the midst of this wild, untamed, encompassing nature which no one has yet managed to soil, exhaust or control.

Immediately after presenting this Wordsworthian vignette, Lawrence makes a sharp contrast between it and scenes one encounters elsewhere and thereupon draws some culturally significant conclusions about this contrast:

> Usually, however, the peasants of the South have left off the costume. Usually it is the invisible soldiers' gray-green cloth, the Italian khaki. Wherever you go, wherever you may be, you see this khaki, this gray-green war-clothing. How many millions of yards of the thick, excellent, but hateful material the Italian Government must have provided I don't know: but enough to cover Italy with a felt carpet, I should think. It is everywhere. It cases the tiny children in stiff and neutral frocks and coats, it covers their extinguished fathers, and sometimes it even encloses the women in its warmth. It is symbolic of the universal grey mist that has come over men, the extinguishing of all bright individuality, the blotting out of all wild singleness. Oh, democracy! Oh, khaki democracy! (p.71)

In addition to possessing the obviously Ruskinian (and Carlylean) contrast of past and present—the one organic and healthy, the other unnatural and destructive—Lawrence's description of his climb through the Sardinian hills also makes an essentially Ruskinian application of an essentially Ruskinian technique.

Like Ruskin he casts himself in the role of the sage who can discern matters of grave importance to his audience in the most unlikely and even apparently trivial contemporary phenomena. Like his Victorian forebear, Lawrence proceeds by performing an act of interpretation which transforms these phenomena into an emblem of contemporary spiritual states of mind and soul. Furthermore, like Ruskin who claimed in *Modern Painters* that his times, not the medieval ones, were the dark ages, he points to the way men clothe themselves to suggest how much his contemporaries have lost—how much the age of Industrialization has taken from man and his environment.[22]

In such passages, as so frequently throughout his writings, Lawrence adopts the tone and strategies of what John Holloway has taught us to call the "Victorian Sage." [23] As I have urged elsewhere, we can take the following as a useful working definition of that kind of nonfiction created by the Victorian sages Carlyle, Ruskin and Arnold and their American contemporary Thoreau:

> It is a form of nonfiction that adapts the techniques of the Victorian sermon, neoclassical satire, classical rhetoric, and Old Testament prophecy to create credibility for the interpretations of contemporary phenomena made by a figure, the sage, who stands apart from his audience and society.
>
> The Victorian sage is, above all else, an interpreter, an exegete, one who can read the Signs of the Times. His essential defining claim is that he understands matters that others do not—and that his understanding is of crucial value to those who see with duller eyes.... By showing the members of his audience that truth resides in unexpected places and that he, and only he, can reveal it to them, the sage convinces them to give a hearing to his views of man, society, and culture that might at first seem eccentric and even insane.[24]

Such self-consciously performed acts of interpretation—I write "performed" because they often unfold as performances in the presence of the reader—frequently produce set-pieces which present some phenomenon emblematically as the embodiment of important truth. For example, in *Twilight in Italy*, Lawrence employs the roadside crucifixes in the book's opening section and the Italian soldier in "The Lemon Gardens" as such emblems, and he makes much the same use of his servant's painful experiences with the revolutionaries in *Mornings in Mexico*.

In addition to such acts of interpretive virtuosity, the sage also characteristically tries to win the assent of his audience to his often apparently outlandish views by a series of techniques that establish his superiority to the audience and its dependence upon him. Techniques, such as careful positioning of himself and his views in relation to those of his audience, redefining key terms and satirizing accepted conventions all serve to create what ancient rhetoricians called *ethos*, the effect of credibility. One of Lawrence's major means of achieving credibility appears in descriptions, which, like those of Ruskin, immediately establish him as one who can see, one who views the external world with sharpened, cleansed perceptions.

Many of those set-pieces of word-painting which characterize both men's writings impress upon the reader that he is in the presence of someone worth listening to who reacts more sensitively, more accurately, and certainly more intensely and interestingly than could the reader himself, even if he were present in the landscape described. Moreover, those passages of description which add characteristically Laurencean elements of physical, semi-conscious awareness to a setting or event, such as the superb description of San Tommaso in *Twilight in Italy*, create a characteristically Laurencean ethos by demonstrating what unique experiential and imaginative truths he has to offer. In other words, such descriptions simultaneously make Lawrence's claim to be a sage and then forcefully substantiate them.

At times Lawrence's creations of what I have termed ethos take the comparatively simple form of drawing the reader's attention to Lawrence as a perceiver, as a man very like the reader. For example, at the beginning of "The Crucifix across the Mountains," that magnificent Ruskinian combination of aesthetic, political, anthropological and religious argument and observation which opens *Twilight in Italy*, he remarks: "I was startled into consciousness one evening, going alone over a marshy place at the foot of the mountain when the sky was pale and unearthly, invisible, and the hills were nearly black" (p. 4). This sentence, which seems merely a casual remark in passing, serves several purposes. First of all, since he tries to win the assent of his reader by convincing him of his observations, such a remark begins with an attempt to convince the reader of his openness, his receptivity, to such phenomena and his suitability for such an enterprise. Perhaps even more important for his purposes, Lawrence, who is here engaged to inform the reader about a particularly interesting and therefore supposedly important perception, provides the autobiographical occasion for his perception, thus rooting it in a kind of personally achieved authenticity, and also reveals to the reader that he, like us, does not always exist in some heightened state of consciousness. In other words, like Montaigne, a master of this technique, he admits his own weakness and his own lapses to convince us that when he tells us something he considers important, he does so with full honesty. Similarly, many of Lawrence's most annoying assertions of selfhood and displays of his own foibles effectively serve to inform the reader that he is being given a supposedly unedited version of the truth. The logic of such a rhetorical strategy seems to follow this path: "If I have repeatedly admitted my limitations, confessed my foolishness, and displayed my shortcomings so openly, so honestly, the reader can be certain that I now give him the full truth." Of course, such premises do not inevitably lead to such conclusions, and, indeed, when Lawrence, like Ruskin, fails to achieve his intended effect, he fails miserably. But, after all, the art of the sage requires its practitioners to take grave rhetorical risks.

Lawrence also employs the techniques of the sage in his fiction. In addition to thus using Ruskinian word-painting to create symbolic settings within which to place his characters, Lawrence also combines such word-painting, as he does in his non-fiction, to create satiric emblems. For example, in *The Rainbow* the description of Tom Brangwen's home perched above a hideously ugly industrial wasteland powerfully sums up—and attacks—the destructions of the modern world against which Ruskin, Lawrence and Lawrence's characters all have to strive in order to preserve life and vitality:

> The place had the strange desolation of a ruin. Colliers hanging about in gangs and groups, or passing along the asphalt pavements heavily to work, seemed not like living people, but like spectres. The rigidity of the blank streets, the homogeneous amorphous sterility of the whole suggested death rather than life. There was no meeting place, no centre, no organic formation. There it lay, like the new foundations of a red-brick confusion rapidly spreading, like a skin-disease.
>
> Just outside of this, on a little hill, was Tom Brangwen's big, red-brick house. It looked from the front upon the edge of the place, a meaningless squalor of ash-pits and closets and irregular rows of the backs of houses, each with its small activity made sordid by barren cohesion with the rest of the small activities. Further off was the great colliery that went night and day. And all around was the country, green with two winding streams, ragged with gorse, and heath, the darker woods in the distance.
>
> The whole place was unreal, just unreal. Even now, when he had been there for two years, Tom Brangwen did not believe in the actuality of the place. It was like some gruesome dream, some ugly, dead, amorphous mood become concrete. . . . The place was a moment of chaos fixed and rigid.

Lawrence's placing of Tom's home within this blighted nature owes much to Ruskin. First, the major Ruskinian theme that modern economics and industrialization embody, not new order, but new chaos informs the entire description. Second, Lawrence, following Ruskin, continually contrasts nature with man and the domesticated, soiled space he has created. Third, this opposition takes the form of what is essentially an allegorical emblem, each detail of which must be read as an indictment of the beings who have created such chaos. Furthermore, the specific placement of Tom Brangwen's home on a hill overlooking the workplace, which is certainly an accurate rendering of many towns in the midlands and industrial north, also seems to derive from Ruskin's "Traffic," which presents a satiric portrait of the industrialist's ideal existence.

In other words, as these few examples suggest, Lawrence drew upon Ruskin for a congeries of complex ideas and techniques which influences the shape, the texture, the feeling of all his writing. Both men were practicing visual artists, and both were controversial, often brilliant critics of both art and society. But, different as were the men and the needs of their ages, they shared a great many ideas, attitudes and emphases, some of which stem from their common Evangelical Protestant tradition. Lawrence's desire to combine the techniques and interests of the word-painter with the mission of the secular prophet makes him, however unexpectedly, a Ruskinian modernist.

CHAPTER FOUR

# Lawrence and George Eliot: The Genesis of *The White Peacock*

## H. M. DALESKI

I

One of the features of Lawrence's achievement as a novelist is the uncanny inwardness of his presentation of women and, particularly, of their sexuality—as in the notable instances of Ursula Brangwen (especially in *The Rainbow*) and Lady Chatterley. We may perhaps best place Lawrence in the tradition of the English novel in this respect if we compare his heroines with those of Jane Austen some hundred years earlier. Sex is a decided factor in Jane Austen—it is, indeed, *the* explosive and disruptive force in the otherwise stable world she depicts, breaking out calamitously in characters such as Lydia Bennet in *Pride and Prejudice* or Maria Bertram (Mrs Rushworth) in *Mansfield Park*—but it is not for heroines. Or not so that we can notice it, for though a Fanny Price or an Emma Woodhouse may be presumed to have sexual needs and desires, the novelist does not allow these to rise to consciousness or overtly to influence behaviour. This tacit differentiation of women into sheep and goats was subsequently extended and sharpened in the work of two other major novelists. Dickens stamped two opposed images of women on the Victorian consciousness in his presentation, at the outset of his career, of the two contrasted young women of *Oliver Twist*, Rose Maylie, the heroine, and Nancy, the prostitute. In his portrayal of Rose, Dickens contrives both to evoke a burgeoning womanhood and to spiritualize it out of existence, epitomizing in her, nearly twenty years before Coventry Patmore put a name to it, an Angel in the House. Home, in Dickens, is no place for lust. That is for the likes of Nancy, a Fallen Woman of the Streets, who exists unmitigatedly in the flesh. And Thackeray was working in the same tradition that produced a Rose and a Nancy, though with a greater subtlety and complexity of characterization, in his representation in *Vanity Fair* of the seemingly angelic, sexless Amelia Sedley as opposed to the demonic, sexy Becky Sharp. When Lawrence speaks of literary images of woman, his account is broader—and racier—but he makes essentially the same kind of distinction:

> The real trouble about women is that they must always go on trying to adapt themselves to men's theories of women, as they always have done. When a woman is thoroughly herself, she is being what her type of man wants her to be. . . . Dickens invented the child–wife, so child–wives have swarmed ever since. He also fished out his version of the chaste Beatrice, a chaste but marriageable Agnes. George Eliot imitated this pattern, and it became confirmed. . . .
>
> There is, also, the eternal secret ideal of men—the prostitute. Lots of women live up to this idea: just because men want them to. . . .
>
> Now the real tragedy is not that women ask and must ask for a pattern of womanhood. The tragedy is not, even, that men give them such abominable patterns, child–wives, little-boy-baby-face girls, perfect secretaries, noble spouses, self-sacrificing mothers, pure women who bring forth children in virgin coldness, prostitutes who just make themselves low, to please the men; all the atrocious patterns of womanhood that men have supplied to woman; patterns all perverted from any real natural fulness of a human being. . . . [T]he one thing [man] won't accept her as is a human being, a real human being of the feminine sex.[1]

Lawrence rightly maintains that the centrally opposed images of woman as Angel or Whore (and their derivatives) are a product, whether directly or indirectly, of the male imagination. And he correctly insists that what the varying images have in common is that they leave the woman out, a woman who has the "real natural fulness of a human being." But he does George Eliot an injustice. It was she, if anyone, who made a concerted effort to reassemble the polarized images and put woman together again. Following the lead given her by Emily Brontë in *Wuthering Heights* and Charlotte Brontë in *Jane Eyre*, it was she, tentatively in her portrayal of Hetty Sorrel in *Adam Bede*, and then magisterially in that of Maggie Tulliver in *The Mill on the Floss* and Dorothea Brooke in *Middlemarch*, who created lasting embodiments of "a real human being of the feminine sex." It would seem to be more than a coincidence of literary history that the challenge to the Dickensian conception of woman came most strongly from women novelists—though in making it they in turn proceeded to polarize the men to whom their heroines are attracted; and Hardy's subsequent rendering of Tess Durbeyfield is as memorably full a portrayal as any they essayed. But the split remained, even though it was now internalized within unitary images of the heroine, and it is not until Lawrence's Ursula Brangwen that we are given a depiction of an achieved wholeness of being.

Lawrence should then be regarded as having been engaged, among other things, in the same enterprise as George Eliot, and the quoted reference to her should accordingly be viewed as an instance of the kind of "misreading" of a precursor that Harold Bloom discusses in *The Anxiety of Influence*, a misreading that is liberating. For I believe that George Eliot was the major initial influence on Lawrence, and that he indeed found himself through her. The signs of her influence are stamped everywhere on his first novel, where we might expect to see them most innocently displayed—to a degree that *The White Peacock* may rewardingly be read as Lawrence's rewriting of *The Mill on the Floss*.

## II

*The White Peacock*, Raney Stanford has remarked, is "generally regarded as the most Hardyesque of any of Lawrence's work, and generally dismissed as derivative therefore. This influence, most of Lawrence's critics agree, is in the description of and in some vague feeling for nature and rural setting that both writers share."[2] A similar view has been reiterated more recently by John Alcorn: "*The White Peacock*, then, reflects the spirit of Hardy on every level of theme and technique. Above all, Lawrence has invested his landscape with those elements of teeming fertility, wild abandon, and secret wisdom which were the hallmarks of Hardy's nature description."[3] It is true that the Hardy-like descriptions of nature most immediately compel attention in Lawrence's first novel—the descriptions are as sharply meticulous and passionately evocative as any comparable passages in Lawrence's later work—but Alcorn's relating of the novel to *Jude the Obscure* (the theme of entrapment in marriage as figured in George Saxton; the supposed modelling of Lettie Beardsall on Sue Bridehead) does not seem to me to illuminate its central concerns. Its provenance should be sought rather in the work of George Eliot. This is not, of course, to deny the influence of Hardy, but I should say it is more significant at a later stage of Lawrence's career, and is indeed directly reflected then in his "Study of Thomas Hardy" (1914).

The opening pages of *The White Peacock* at once reveal small but suggestive links with *The Mill on the Floss*. Where George Eliot's main setting is Dorlcote Mill, Lawrence's is Strelley Mill; and his setting is the more notable in that it is a composite location, merging the real-life Haggs Farm (home of the Chambers family, the prototypes of the Saxtons in the novel) and the nearby Felley Mill Farm. Jessie Chambers has described how from the stackyard of the Haggs "the land dipped to the valley where we could see in the hollow the red roofs of Felley Mill";[4] but in the novel it is the Saxton farm which becomes "the Mill"—as if it were a mill which had a hold on Lawrence's imagination. Where the narrator of *The Mill on the Floss* begins her narrative by musing on the past, "dreaming" that she is "standing on the bridge in front of Dorlcote Mill, as it looked one February afternoon many years ago,"[5] Cyril Beardsall, the narrator of *The White Peacock* (who proves to be a semi-absentee narrator, possessed of a striking talent for describing events at which he is not present), begins his narrative by telling his friend George he has been thinking how "the place" he has just described "[seems] old, brooding over its past."[6] And both narrators, the one in her reverie and the other in fact, start by staring into the mill-ponds, she "in love with moistness" and experiencing "a dreamy deafness, which seems to heighten the peacefulness of the scene" (*MF*, 8), he taken by how "intensely still" everything is, for "the whole place [is] gathered in the musing of old age" (*WP*, 13). For good measure, *The Mill on the Floss* even has its own peacock, a less portentous creature, no doubt, than that imaged by Lawrence, but there nonetheless (*MF*, 78, 84, 271).

In addition, there is external testimony that George Eliot and *The Mill on the Floss* were in Lawrence's mind when he began writing his first novel. Jessie Chambers has told us that "Lawrence adored *The Mill on the Floss*"; that "Maggie Tulliver was his favourite heroine. He used to say that the smooth branches of the beech trees (which he especially admired) reminded him of Maggie Tulliver's arms"; and that he consciously modelled *The White Peacock* on George Eliot's work:

Lawrence now began to talk definitely of writing. He said he thought he should try a novel, and wanted me to try to write one too, so that we could compare notes.

"The usual plan is to take two couples and develop their relationships," he said. "Most of George Eliot's are on that plan. Anyhow, I don't want a plot, I should be bored with it. I shall try two couples for a start."[7]

Emily Saxton and Cyril Beardsall are presumably one of the couples Lawrence intended writing about, but in the event their relationship is not "developed," as prescribed. In the published novel it is no more than vaguely adumbrated—these characters were to await their more vital reincarnation as Miriam Leivers and Paul Morel in *Sons and Lovers*—and the action is set in motion by the dynamics of a triangle, not of coupling, since Lettie Beardsall is attracted to George Saxton when she is already involved with Leslie Tempest. Lawrence's actual structural pattern, that is to say, does in fact follow that of George Eliot in *The Mill on the Floss*; for once the long and loving delineation of the childhood of Maggie and her brother Tom is completed and the book moves belatedly to its main concern in the depiction of Maggie's adult relationships,[8] Stephen Guest and Lucy Deane prove to be no more substantial a "couple" than Cyril and Emily, and the motivating principle of the action is Maggie's triangular relationships with Stephen and Philip Wakem. It is notable that Lawrence also incorporates a relationship between a sister and brother to mediate between the relationships of the various couples and lovers, as does George Eliot, though the depiction of Lettie's relations with Cyril is nowhere near as vivid or as important as that of Maggie's with Tom.

What seems to have caught Lawrence's imagination, however, and what was to prove to be so decisive a factor in his own development as a novelist, was the underlying significance of the love-triangle in *The Mill on the Floss*. Philip and Stephen, the two men to whom Maggie is attracted, are not only presented as thoroughgoing opposites but (as remains to be discussed) embody opposed tendencies within Maggie herself. In her relationship with each of her lovers, she negates or suppresses one part of herself, which is activated in relation to the other man. The opposition within the self of the heroine is thus concretized in the opposition between the two lovers, just as her self-division is externalized in her attraction to both men—and in her ultimate incapacity to choose between them. What her story dramatizes, therefore, is her inability to reconcile the opposed forces within herself. And Lawrence follows the same pattern in his love-triangle in *The White Peacock*. Leslie and George are as strongly opposed as Philip and Stephen; and, I shall argue, figure an opposition which is embodied in Lettie, and which is also strikingly similar in nature to that presented in the earlier novel. Lettie is as much torn between Leslie and George as Maggie between her lovers. Though she, unlike Maggie, does finally choose one man, for ten years she is unable to give the other up, and her story is similarly one of self-division.[9]

Lawrence would seem to have been impelled to follow the pattern laid down by George Eliot in *The Mill on the Floss* for three main reasons. First, it exemplified a simple but effective method of organizing a novel. The love-triangle enabled him both to dramatize his heroine's self-division and to project the sort of opposition he was concerned with in his presentation of her lovers—and at the same time to contain the narrative within a unifying configuration. Second, it offered a tangible means of realizing the aim he wished to set for himself as a novelist, even though he once again "misread" George Eliot in formulating this aim—as Jessie Chambers's report of one of their conversations indicates:

> A fragment of conversation about writing and writers comes back to me. We were in the wood....
> "You see, it was really George Eliot who started it all," Lawrence was saying in the deliberate way he had of speaking when he was trying to work something out in his own mind. "And how wild they all were with her for doing it. It was she who started putting all the action inside. Before, you know, with Fielding and the others, it had been outside. Now I wonder which is right?"
> I always found myself most interested in what people thought and experienced within themselves, so I ventured the opinion that George Eliot had been right.
> "I wonder if she was," Lawrence replied thoughtfully. "You know I can't help thinking there ought to be a bit of both."[10]

The love-triangle in *The Mill on the Floss* clearly offers a model of how to put "a bit of both" in a novel, how to incorporate both the "inside" and the "outside," for it figures the externalization of inner conflict. It was a model which Lawrence made his own in the first stage of his career, adopting it not only in *The White Peacock* but more memorably in *Sons and Lovers*. In *Sons and Lovers* the protagonist is a man—it is perhaps a further indication of the hold Lawrence's "favourite heroine" had on him that in his first novel the character with whom he is most significantly identified should have been a woman—but Paul Morel's relations with Miriam Leivers and Clara Dawes follow the same pattern and have the same kind of import. It is notable, however, that whereas George Eliot throughout her career continued to combine inner and outer views, nowhere more strikingly perhaps than in *Middlemarch*, in the end it was Lawrence himself who, in *The Rainbow*, made one of the most sustained efforts in the English novel to put all the action inside. He called the method he employed in *The Rainbow* "exhaustive," and must have felt he had fully exploited its possibilities in this work, for in *Women in Love* and subsequent novels he returned to a more even balance between inner and outer worlds.

Third, we may assume Lawrence was especially struck by the love-triangle in *The Mill on the Floss* because it spoke to his own deepest experience as a young man. The broad opposition it projects is one that he grew up with, for it is not dissimilar to that represented by the dire clash between his parents, which he was later to chronicle in the description of the marriage of Mr and Mrs Morel in *Sons and Lovers*. And the self-division of the heroine of George Eliot's novel made vivid a condition that he himself was heir to, a condition that he first attempted to objectify and grapple with in his portrayal of Lettie. It proved to be an attempt that left him with an abiding sense of individual duality as an ontological principle and so as a rule of characterization, and it became his life's work to seek for a means of reconciling opposed forces within the self, however they were variously defined. It also left him not only with a heroine but a world divided in two, for in time he was roundly to declare that "everything that exists, even a stone, has two sides to its nature."[11]

### III

In her childhood Maggie Tulliver enjoys a notable wholeness of being though the opposed elements within her are sharply depicted: on the one hand, she is constantly pictured as a young animal, being compared to a Shetland pony and a Skye terrier and so on; on the other, she is shown to have a challengingly keen mind, and is so quick-witted that her father fears she is "too 'cute for a woman" (*MF*, 12). Animal-like vitality and intellectuality, however, coexist in her quite comfortably, neither in any way frustrating the free expression of the other. It is as an adult and in her relations with men that she falls into self-division. Lettie Beardsall is an adult when we meet her, and from the outset her self-division is apparent in her responses to the two men she is interested in. The opposing forces in Lettie are remarkably similar to those in Maggie, though the opposition in her case is perhaps best described, if we follow Lawrencean terminology, as one between mental consciousness and blood-consciousness. Lettie, like Maggie, is a woman with a mind. Though she is proud of her physical appearance, even a little vain, she seems to place the highest value on her mind (*WP*, 40); and as a mature hostess she is said to "overflow" with "clever speeches and rapid, brilliant observations" (*WP*, 322). At the same time, she abundantly possesses "blood-being," has a natural capacity, that is, for untrammelled existence in the flesh, and it is this (as well as "the subtle sympathies of her artist's soul") that is revealed in "her poise and harmonious movement" (*WP*, 117). It is also apparent in the way she is at one with nature, "[glinting] on like a flower" when she moves "brightly through the green hazels" (*WP*, 21).

When Maggie is drawn to Philip Wakem, it is clear that his appeal is to her intellect. He is in many ways a kindred spirit, is himself a Maggie, as it were, with all animality thoroughly tamed, if not quite left out. During the year that they meet secretly he gives her much-needed intellectual companionship and stimulation, but he himself unwittingly indicates what the inevitable result for her of a prolonged association with him would be when he laments the "benumbing and cramping" of her nature which he says is the consequence of her self-imposed "rule of renunciation" (*MF*, 284, 287). For Philip's humpback, his physical deficiency, ensures that "the thought of his being her lover never [enters] her mind" (*MF*, 289). When he finally confesses he loves her, she tacitly allows him to believe she is ready to return his love; and it is at this point that she begins the willed negation of one half of her being which thereafter characterizes her relationship with him.

Maggie registers that a love relationship with Philip will demand a "sacrifice" of her, but it is one that she initially believes she will be glad to make. It goes against the grain, however, as becomes evident when her brother Tom compels her to agree not to see Philip again:

she becomes conscious then of "a certain dim background of relief in the forced separation," and the narrator's suggestion that this is "surely ... only because the sense of a deliverance from concealment [is] welcome at any cost" (*MF*, 305) as surely emphasizes the hidden nature of her relief. Some two years later, when Lucy Deane undertakes to arrange for her to marry Philip, Maggie is startled into an involuntary betrayal of her physical shrinking from him: she "[tries] to smile, but [shivers], as if she [feels] a sudden chill" (*MF*, 338). She persists, however, in declaring her wish to marry him, and maintains that this "would be the best and highest lot" for her (*MF*, 384), seeming to admit to herself that it is a lower, inferior self that has impelled her towards Stephen Guest.

With one part of him Lawrence would seem to affirm such a view:

> The little cripple in *Mill on the Floss* was strong—but a woman despised his frailty. Pah—I hate women's heroes. At the bottom women love the brute in man best, like a great shire stallion makes one's heart beat.[12]

It is notable, therefore, that Leslie Tempest, who is the equivalent figure to Philip in the love-triangle of *The White Peacock*, is given a firm physicality. He has a "fine, lithe physique, suggestive of much animal vigour," his "person" is "exceedingly attractive"; and one is said to feel pleasure when one watches him "move about" (*WP*, 59–60). But his relationship with Lettie is nonetheless founded on the word. Banter is a feature of their relations; and when they make love, they characteristically make words, he even asking her on one occasion what she is "making so many words about" (*WP*, 105). Leslie says he thinks "there's more in the warm touch of a soft body than in a prayer" and declares he will "pray with kisses," but what more immediately seems to attract him to Lettie is her cleverness: "you are clever, you are rare," he announces with delight when she embroiders one of his allusions (*WP*, 103–104). If he is able to titillate her mind, however, he is unable in the irrational and mysterious ways of blood-being to warm her blood, and he is forced to recognize that to him she is "a cold little lover" (*WP*, 101). It is not Leslie but the flattering self-image he can command for her through his social position that kindles Lettie.

Lettie becomes engaged to Leslie, and during the period of the engagement they sleep together. When they meet the next day, she is "angry" with him and makes "a swift gesture of repulsion"; but it is her own hands that she says "disclaim" her and which she "can't bear the sight of," and her own hand which she "hides ... swiftly against her skirt" when she catches sight of it (*WP*, 204–205). Lettie, that is, is filled with self-disgust, and we are to infer that, after all her hesitations in regard to Leslie, what she has now discovered—what her "blood" has now made incontrovertibly clear to her—is that she does not love him and cannot respond physically to him. Yet she is now doubly his. She does subsequently make an effort to break with him, telling him that they cannot be "flesh of one flesh," but by then he is recovering from serious injury as a result of a motor accident, and when he responds by betraying an utter dependence on her, his unmanning distress is too much for her. She puts her arms round him and finally commits herself to him. But what the price of her support of him—of such an abrogation of the blood—is likely to be is intimated by the end of the scene: "Oh—do you want to go away from me again?" Leslie suddenly asks; and she replies, "No—only my arm is dead," and she draws it "from beneath him, standing up, swinging it, smiling because it [hurts] her" (*WP*, 227–228). It is almost as if Lettie enacts the "benumbing and cramping" that is implicit in Maggie's relationship with Philip. And though Jessie Chambers reports that Lawrence declared George Eliot had "gone and spoilt [*The Mill on the Floss*] half way through" because he "could not forgive the marriage of the vital Maggie Tulliver to the cripple Philip," saying, "It was wrong, wrong. She should never have made her do it";[13] he makes his heroine do what Maggie of course did not do, for Lettie marries Leslie, whereas Maggie is drawn away from Philip to Stephen.

In contrast to Philip, Stephen Guest (like Maggie) abundantly possesses bodily potency and a rich physical vitality. It is to his physical force—and attractiveness—that Maggie responds, as he to hers, each becoming "oppressively conscious of the other's presence, even to the finger-ends." It seems also as if George Eliot is evoking a Lawrencean blood-consciousness here—and then again: "Maggie only felt that life was revealing something quite new to her; and she was absorbed in the direct, immediate experience, without any energy left for taking account of it and reasoning about it." She is also said to have "no distinct thought—only the sense of a presence like that of a closely hovering broad-winged bird in the darkness" (*MF*, 352, 355). Yet when Stephen passionately declares his love for her, Maggie rejects him.

At one point during the exchange between Stephen and Maggie at her aunt Moss's, she is said to look at him "like a lovely wild animal timid and struggling under caresses" (*MF*, 393). The simile vividly suggests his power to call to life in her what she has repressed for so long; but their relationship and attraction to each other are entirely on a physical level. When she, therefore, insists that she remains tied to Philip while admitting she loves Stephen, it would seem this is not only a matter of principle: Maggie, we realize, needs and wants both men, wants Philip too for what Stephen cannot give her. Wanting both, she is finally unable to choose one. Pulled in two directions at once, she is incapable of resolving her conflict. The incapacity declares itself in the way she renounces Stephen in the same breath that she confesses she loves him (*MF*, 394).

What it means to Maggie to give Stephen up is powerfully suggested by her response to the letter (written some two months after she has left him at Mudport) in which he begs to be allowed to come to her:

> When Maggie first read this letter she felt as if her real temptation had only just begun. At the entrance of the chill dark cavern, we turn with unworn courage from the warm light; but how, when we have trodden far in the damp darkness, and have begun to be faint and weary—how, if there is a sudden opening above us, and we are invited back again to the life-nourishing day? The leap of natural longing from under the pressure of pain is so strong, that all less immediate motives are likely to be forgotten—till the pain has been escaped from. (*MF*, 449–450)

The dark cavern evokes a tomb; and indeed Maggie has condemned herself to a kind of living death in choosing to be without either Philip or Stephen. Immediately prior to this she seems almost to have lost the will to carry on: "she must begin a new life, in which she would have to rouse herself to receive new impressions—and she was so unspeakably, sickeningly weary!" (*MF*, 449). The "sudden opening" above her which Stephen's letter makes in the cavern thus offers her a chance to rise from the tomb. The "leap of natural longing" to escape from pain which possesses her is also the leap of the lovely wild animal which Stephen again stirs into being and would make its own bid for life.

But, in a culminating instance of Maggie's self-division, the animal is negated by mind: "her mind [recoils]," we are told, and swings her back to her old position (*MF*, 450). Her decision to stand by her renunciation of Stephen may be viewed as a climactic exercise of restraint on her part, the sort of restraint that signifies a truly civilized response to life and an achieved maturity. That would seem to be the view the novelist expects us to take. But what we are also shown is that the decision places Maggie firmly back in the cavern. Facing a life without both Stephen and Philip, she may determine to cleave once again to Thomas à Kempis and bear her cross "till death," but she is in fact reduced to the kind of despair that knows and wants only death, to a despair that can issue only in what Philip once called a "long suicide." It is precisely at this point that the flood begins, but its advent, though carefully prepared for, comes across as sentimentally contrived. In the flood scenes Maggie is granted an access of strength, and with a renewed wholeness of being evocative of her childhood, she rescues Tom and is reunited with him before they drown together—but not even this ending can offset the impression of the irreparable self-division, of the "cry of self-despair" with which she opts for the cavern and which leaves her wanting only to "[bury] her sorrow-stricken face" as her soul goes out to "the Unseen Pity" that will be with her "to the end" (*MF*, 451).

Lettie is as powerfully drawn to George as Maggie to Stephen. In both cases it is the woman who stirs the man to life. Before Maggie appears on the scene, Stephen is presented as a lethargic fop, whose "diamond ring, attar of roses, and air of nonchalant leisure, at twelve o'clock in the day, are the graceful and odoriferous result of the largest oil-mill and the most extensive wharf in St Ogg's" (*MF*, 316). Cyril, at the start of his narrative, tells George that his "life is nothing else but a doss," and declares he will "laugh when somebody jerks [him] awake" (*WP*, 13). The awakening follows speedily: when Lettie visits the Mill and plays "a love song" for him at the piano—it is notable that the relationship of Maggie and Stephen likewise develops in scenes at the piano at Lucy's home—George is roused to look at her "with glowing brown eyes, as if in hesitating challenge," and she answers with "a blue blaze of her eyes" (*WP*, 27). If she is compelled by his physical presence, however, she is also made fearful by it, for it "[scatters] her words like startled birds" (*WP*, 26), seeming for a time to annul mental consciousness. On another occasion, when he looks at her with "wide and vivid" eyes, she first shrinks back, "as if flame [has] leaped towards her face," but then returns his gaze and they both "tremble with a fierce sensation that [fills] their veins with fluid, fiery electricity"; both then feel "the blood beating madly in their necks" (*WP*, 43–44). Lettie's relationship with George, in contradistinction to that with Leslie which is based on the word, is anchored in the blood, but she is not willing to submit to its mad beat. In the end she seems to opt for the mind as a *modus operandi*: "she, who had always been so rippling in thoughtless life, sat down in the window-sill to think...." (*WP*, 92). The result is that she chooses Leslie as a clearly better match.

But she still remains drawn to George, and even intimates her doubts about the choice she has made. "No, I won't come down [to tea]," she says to George, "—let me say farewell—*jamque Vale!* Do you remember how Eurydice sank back into Hell?" (*WP*, 246). On the same occasion—it is shortly before her marriage to Leslie—she suggests to George that they walk together into the wood. She repeatedly seeks physical contact with him, ruffling his hair, leaving her land lying on his knee, leaning softly against him; roused, George passionately declares his love:

> "No, Lettie," he pleaded, with terror and humility. "No, Lettie; don't go. What should I do with my life? Nobody would love you like I do—and what should I do with my love for you?—hate it and fear it, because it's too much for me?"
> She turned and kissed him gratefully. He then took her in a long, passionate embrace, mouth to mouth. In the end it had so wearied her that she could only wait in his arms till he was too tired to hold her. He was trembling already.
> "Poor Meg!" she murmured to herself dully, her sensations having become vague.
> He winced, and the pressure of his arms slackened. She loosened his hands, and rose half dazed from her seat by him. She left him, while he sat dejected, raising no protest. (*WP*, 248–249)

This is the climactic moment of Lettie's relationship with George. She is now given a chance to climb out of the Hell into which she feels she is sinking—just as Maggie in relation to Stephen has the opportunity to leap out of the dark cavern in which she finds herself and return to "the life-nourishing day." But Lettie allows the chance to slip through her fingers because she wills herself into being deaf to what her blood-consciousness tells her, just as, analogously, Maggie allows her mind to recoil and swing her back into the cavern. Accordingly, Lettie does not heed George's appeal even though she is overcome by his embrace—and though she is as much overcome by the knowledge the passionate kiss conveys. "Poor Meg," she says, registering the unhappiness that George, loving her as he does with all his being, will doom Meg to by marrying her. And "poor Leslie" she might have murmured as well, for she has not been an unwilling partner in the embrace, has even provoked it, showing unequivocally how much she wants George even while insisting she is bound to Leslie. Though George characteristically "slackens" and accepts her departure, she must be assumed to submerge the truth of that kiss in her sense of the superior attainments, social position and wealth of Leslie, for she proceeds to marry him in spite of it.

At this point Lawrence may be regarded, in Harold Bloom's terms, as executing a *clinamen* or "swerve" in relation to his precursor. The ending of *The Mill on the Floss* is unsatisfactory because, in effect, George Eliot evades a full confrontation of the issues her fiction has raised. The "long suicide" that is implicit in Maggie's condition when she rejects Stephen's appeal is transformed into an heroic death; and what her death means for both Philip and Stephen is not pursued, though we are told that they visit her grave and that "one of them" visits it again "with a sweet face beside him . . . years after" (*MF*, 457). What Lawrence does, devoting about one-third of his novel to this, is to explore the consequences for all three protagonists of Letttie's decision to marry Leslie.

An immediate indication of Lettie's lack of fulfilment in her marriage is that she can "never quite let [George] be," and that she is subject to "a driving force" that impels her "against her will to interfere in his life" (*WP*, 336). Though she desists from visiting him at his home after he is married because Meg proves to be "too antagonistic," she keeps up the friendship with him "in spite of all things," and he visits her at Highclose "perhaps once in a fortnight." Some ten years after the announcement of her engagement to Leslie, she seems to be no less engaged by George; and while she lets Leslie "forget her birthday" and so be away from home on the occasion, "for some unknown reason, she [lets] the intelligence slip to George," whom she invites to dinner. And ten years after the engagement, they still have much the same effect on each other (*WP*, 339–340).

George says that he looks "to marriage" to set him busy on his "house of life, something whole and complete, of which it will supply the design" (*WP*, 274); but the very foundation of his life is undermined when he marries Meg though still in love with Lettie. Years later he tacitly admits his responsibility for the failure of his marriage, unknowingly establishing a parallel between himself and Lettie in relation to her husband: "I can't give [Meg] any of the real part of me," he tells Cyril, "the vital part that she wants—I can't, any more than you could give kisses to a stranger" (*WP*, 342–343). The result is that Meg, who is "secure in her high maternity," humiliates him and is "hostile to his wishes" (*WP*, 314); and he feels "like a vacuum . . . all loose in the middle of a space of darkness, that's pressing on you" (*WP*, 328). Without marriage as a firm base from which to operate, moreover, George cannot really make a success of anything else. At first he sets out to make money, but, though he becomes quite well-to-do, his money-making is at bottom an escape from an inner nullity, from the vacuum of his being. Becoming disillusioned with mere prosperity, he begins to work for the socialist cause, but his political ardour soon peters out. In the end he lets everything go, and subsides into a gradual drunken deterioration. Even the fire of his "evil-drunk" rages soon dies out, and he sinks in the prime of his life into a feeble alcoholic passivity. When Cyril sees him for the last time, he is "lamentably decayed," leaning against a gate "like a tree that is falling, going soft and pale and rotten, clammy with small fungi" (*WP*, 366–367).

Leslie, like George, also goes in for public life after his marriage, becoming a county councillor and speaking authoritatively as a mine owner on economic questions of the day; but we are to understand that he too does not excel as a public man. This would also seem to be attributable to the nature of his marriage—Lettie encourages him in his political ambitions because "it [relieves] her of him" (*WP*, 339)—though we are not told much about his view of it. Cyril states that after his marriage Leslie seems to "[lose] his assertive self-confidence," and almost at once reports that "Lettie and he [have] separate rooms" when they stay at Woodside (*WP*, 296). As Cyril sees it, the marriage for Leslie, far from being vitalizing, is notable for the ease with which he makes it non-existent: "As Lettie was always a very good wife, Leslie adored her when he had the time, and when he had not, forgot her comfortably" (*WP*, 330).

The change in Lettie after her marriage is first apparent when she makes no attempt to conceal a general sense of disillusionment, and Cyril offers the following summing up of her condition:

> Having reached that point in a woman's career when most, perhaps all of the things in life seem worthless and insipid, she had determined to put up with it, to ignore her own self, to empty her own potentialities into the vessel of another or others, and to live her life at second hand. This peculiar abnegation of self is the resource of a woman for the escaping of the responsibilities of her own development. Like a nun, she puts over her living face a veil, as a sign that the woman no longer exists for herself: she is the servant of God, of some man, or her children, or may be of some cause. As a servant, she is no longer responsible for herself, which would make her terrified and lonely. Service is light and easy. . . . [Lettie] had . . . now determined to abandon the charge of herself to serve her children. (*WP*, 323–324)

Cyril formulates his view of Lettie as a general proposition about the life of women, but her disillusionment is clearly personal, and as clearly to be attributed to the vacuity of her marriage. Her condition, pulled as she still is between the man she has married and the man she cannot let be, is analogous to that of Maggie, torn irrevocably between Philip and Stephen; and, like Maggie, she would seem to be poised for breakdown. Lettie does not overtly break down, but she falls apart at the innermost core of her being—and in effect ceases to be, certainly as Lawrence understands meaningful being. The central indication of this is her determination "to empty her own potentialities into the vessel of another or others": Lettie allows herself to lapse into the life of her child, permitting the core of the self to dissolve, as it were, and pouring herself into her son. The result is her own vital inanition, and a negation of self that constitutes her "long suicide" as she lives her life at second hand and abandons "the charge of herself to serve her children." Such a sacrifice of self is a denial of "the responsibilities of her own development"—as she has previously denied her sexual being.

In the end Lettie tells Cyril that she has "nothing at all in her life," and declares it is "a barren futility": "I hope I shall have another child next spring," she writes; "there is only that to take away the misery of this torpor. I seem full of passion and energy, and it all fizzles out in day-to-day domestics" (*WP*, 330). When, after ten years of continued flirtation, George forces the issue, insisting "it must be one way or another," she "coldly" opts for a final parting

(*WP*, 345)—but then she again defrauds herself, and her own blood is now virtually stilled: "Lettie's heart would quicken in answer to only one pulse, the easy, light ticking of the baby's blood" (*WP*, 357).

It is in his having gone beyond George Eliot in his first novel that Lawrence may be said to have found himself through her—to have discovered, that is, some of the basic thematic material which he was steadily to mine in his future career. The two bad marriages with which *The White Peacock* concludes come to serve as a springboard. First, the failure of both George and Leslie, but particularly George, to make anything significant of their lives concretizes what Lawrence was to declare in direct expository terms (and to dramatize again and again in his fiction) to be the dependence of man's "purposive activity," whether individual or collective, on sexual fulfilment:

> Sex holds any *two* people together, but it tends to disintegrate society, unless it is subordinated to the great dominating male passion of collective *purpose*.
> But when the sex passion submits to the great purposive passion, then you have fullness. And no great purposive passion can endure long unless it is established upon the fulfilment in the vast majority of individuals of the true sexual passion.[14]

Second, George (and not Annable the gamekeeper, as often asserted, though he clearly has his links with Mellors in *Lady Chatterley's Lover*) becomes an archetypal Lawrence character, leading in his vivid physical being and its squalid drunken extinction to Walter Morel in *Sons and Lovers*, and in his money-making as an escape from an inner vacuity to both Gerald Crich in *Women in Love* and Clifford Chatterley; just as Leslie, the mine owner, in his childlike dependence on a woman leads in his own way to both Gerald and Clifford. Third, the women who remain unfulfilled in their marriages become archetypal too. Meg, who is denied "the real part" of George even though she proceeds to bear him five children, leads to Anna Brangwen in *The Rainbow* in the high maternity that is implacably hostile to her husband. And Lettie, who sacrifices herself in order to serve her children, leads not only to Mrs Morel in *Sons and Lovers* but to Lawrence's insistence on the perniciousness of all such sacrifice of self, and to his exploration of the effects of such ministrations on the children who are its beneficiaries.

But above all *The White Peacock* initiates Lawrence's pursuit of an alternative outcome to the kind of self-division Lettie exemplifies. In the figure of Paul Morel in *Sons and Lovers*, Lawrence was to depict such a condition even more profoundly and vividly, and the crucial development occurs at the end of that novel. Unlike Lettie, Paul does not choose the "halfness" or "partness" which is offered him, for he rejects both Miriam Leivers and Clara Dawes, seeking a wholeness of being away from both of them. And unlike Maggie's rejection of Philip and Stephen, his is positive, for whereas she knowingly opts for the dark cavern, he turns his back on the darkness and walks towards "the faintly humming, glowing town, quickly." With *Sons and Lovers* behind him, Lawrence was ready for the attempt to determine how the two opposed modes of consciousness could be integrated in a unified self—was ready, that is, for his Ursula Brangwen.

CHAPTER FIVE

# Lawrence and Hardy

## ROBERT LANGBAUM

The best source of comparison between Thomas Hardy and D. H. Lawrence is Lawrence's curious little book *Study of Thomas Hardy* (the *Study* is curious in its mixture of literary criticism with metaphysics, autobiography, cultural history and other things). In the *Study*, Lawrence implicitly acknowledges Hardy as his master. Hardy takes on new relevance and stature when we realize that he is the principal influence on one of the two most innovative, twentieth-century English-speaking novelists (the other is Joyce); and we understand Lawrence better when we realize that he differs only in degree from Hardy and when we can trace the roots of Lawrence's art back through Hardy to George Eliot and Wordsworth.

To some extent Lawrence's relation to Hardy illustrates Harold Bloom's theory of influence, in that Lawrence in the *Study* partly misreads and rewrites Hardy's novels as a way of arriving at his own art. But the *Study* shows no sign of what Bloom calls "the anxiety of influence," in that Lawrence is not out to defeat Hardy—he wants to complete him, to continue his direction, to fulfill the implications of Hardy's art that Hardy as a Victorian could not fulfill. It is true that Lawrence so assimilates Hardy that "one can," to borrow Bloom's words "believe, for startled moments" that Lawrence is being "imitated"[1] by Hardy. Such absorption is not, however, necessarily aggressive; it can be a way of learning all one can from the precursor before going on to take the inevitable next step to finding one's own identity as a writer.

Although Lawrence criticizes Hardy for allowing his metaphysic or moral judgment to outweigh his sympathy for his convention-breaking characters, he writes about Hardy's novels with such affectionate understanding that his admiration is what we remember.

"Nothing in [Hardy's] work," says Lawrence, "is so pitiable as his clumsy efforts to push events into line with his theory of being, and to make calamity fall on those who represent the principle of Love. . . . His feeling, his instinct, his sensuous understanding is, however, apart from his metaphysic, very great and deep, deeper than that, perhaps, of any other English novelist."[2] The same criticism—that he is weak in metaphysic, strong in sensibility—is often made against Lawrence.

If we recall at what point in his career Lawrence wrote the *Study of Hardy*, we realize that Lawrence places himself in Hardy's line in order to understand himself as a novelist, to understand where he comes from and where he is going. It was on 15 July 1914, a moment of triumph, when he had married Frieda and sent off *The Rainbow* to Methuen, that Lawrence asked a friend to lend him Hardy's novels because he hoped "to write a little book on Hardy's people." August was a month of reverses. Methuen returned the manuscript and the war broke out. On 5 September Lawrence wrote to his agent: "What a miserable world. What colossal idiocy, this war. Out of sheer rage I've begun my book about Thomas Hardy."[3] The book on Hardy was conceived, however, in a moment of happiness; and there is no rage in it. The *Study of Hardy* is, like the final version of *The Rainbow* to which it provides the skeletal structure, optimistic about the possibility for the evolution of human consciousness through the right kind of marriage.

The apparent digressiveness of the *Study* has led most readers (and Lawrence himself at times) to conclude that Hardy is a mere pretext for Lawrence's expression of his own philosophy, and that the three chapters dealing directly with Hardy (chapters III, V, IX) have little to do with the other ten chapters. I want to argue, instead, that the *Study* does hang together, that the metaphysic no less than the criticism derives from Lawrence's understanding of Hardy's novels. "Normally, the centre, the turning pivot, of a man's life," writes Lawrence in the *Study*, "is his sex-life, the centre and swivel of his being is the sexual act."[4] Hardy thought so too; he is the first Victorian novelist, perhaps the first English novelist, to have thought so. That is why he was always in trouble with the bowdlerizers and censors. Lawrence says that in the division of human life between the purpose of self-preservation and the sexual-creative purpose (the distinction corresponds to Freud's between the reality and pleasure principles), Hardy's people are mainly committed to the sexual-creative purpose. Thus Lawrence's metaphysic—which sees all life as sexual and equates sexuality with spirit—can be said to derive from his understanding of Hardy. Writers of course have always dealt with sex. The difference in Hardy and especially in Lawrence is the centrality of sex—the fact that sex is self-justifying, that it is not subject to judgment by other values but is indeed the source of other values. The ironic subtitle, *A Pure Woman*, to *Tess of the d'Urbervilles*, challenges the quite opposite conventional judgment of Tess.

Far from being a digression, then, the chapters on the metaphysic—especially those that account for our cultural and psychic history by the necessary opposition of male and female principles—are necessary for an understanding of Lawrence's readings of Hardy's novels. Lawrence's valid insights outweigh his misreadings, making him Hardy's best critic, the first to understand Hardy's innovativeness and relevance to the twentieth century. We can never read Hardy in the same way once we have encountered Lawrence in the *Study* and the novels, and have come to realize that Lawrence took from Hardy the great new subjects of sex and the unconscious.

Lawrence's *Study of Thomas Hardy* influenced the final version of *The Rainbow*, as is amply demonstrated by Mark Kinkead-Weekes, who shows that Lawrence needed to write the *Study* in order to find out what he had been up to in the vast draft, called *The Sisters*,[5] which by the time of the *Study* was separated into *The Rainbow* and what would be called *Women in Love*. Lawrence, according to Kinkead-Weekes, learned two main things from Hardy's example: he learned the necessity for and the danger of a metaphysic. Every great novel, Lawrence writes in the *Study*, "must have the background or the structural skeleton of some theory of being, some metaphysic." Hardy anticipated the modernists in being the first Victorian novelist and poet to feel the need of a system—a system he finally worked out in his mammoth, still-born epic poem *The Dynasts* (1903–08). It is because of Hardy's metaphysic that Lawrence places him on a level with Tolstoi; but their metaphysic, says Lawrence, damaged the art of both novelists when it overcame their "living sense of being.... The metaphysic must always subserve the artistic purpose beyond the artist's conscious aim. Otherwise the novel becomes a treatise." Lawrence seems to be thinking of the defeat by society of Hardy's Tess and Tolstoi's Anna Karenina when he goes on to say that "Hardy's metaphysic is something like Tolstoi's. 'There is no reconciliation between Love and the Law,' says Hardy. 'The spirit of Love must always succumb before the blind, stupid, but overwhelming power of the Law.'"[6]

In determining that "The metaphysic must always subserve the artistic purpose beyond the artist's conscious aim," Lawrence arrives at a theory of the proper subordination of conscious to unconscious intention. This connects with the other main thing that Lawrence probably learned from Hardy—a new sense of unconscious or impersonal identity. Lawrence found in Hardy, says Kinkead-Weekes, "a language in which to conceive the impersonal forces he saw operating within and between human beings," and this helped him understand "what the novel he had been trying to write was really *about*."[7] It was about the new sense of identity, which is why Lawrence felt impelled, as a way of retracing his steps for the sake of understanding, to write about Hardy's *people*.

Hardy's new sense of identity is clearest, Lawrence implies, in the way he relates characters to landscape. In *The Return of the Native*, the people

> are one year's accidental crop. . . . The Heath persists. Its body is strong and fecund, it will bear many more crops beside this. . . . The contents of the small lives are spilled and wasted. There is savage satisfaction in it: for so much more remains to come, such a black, powerful fecundity is working there that what does it matter?[8]

The Heath is the external, impersonal identity of which the people are passing manifestations.

Out of this passage and the *Study's* metaphysic of female and male principles emerge the great opening passages of *The Rainbow* (written after the *Study*),[9] where the Brangwens are portrayed as passing manifestations of the fecund landscape. The men are absorbed by organic connection with the female earth, by "blood-intimacy": "the pulse of the blood of the teats of the cows beat into the pulse of the hands of the men"; whereas the women look upward to the male church tower and aspire to a life of spirit.[10] The sexualization of landscape derives from Hardy—from the voluptuous landscapes in *Far from the Madding Crowd* and from passages in *Tess* like this one:

> Amid the oozing fatness and warm ferments of the Froom Vale, at a season when the rush of juices could almost be heard below the

hiss of fertilization, it was impossible that the most fanciful love should not grow passionate. The ready bosoms existing there were impregnated by their surroundings.[11]

Hardy and Lawrence sexualize Wordsworth's living landscapes.

That is because Hardy and Lawrence are Darwinians. "Man has a purpose," says Lawrence in a statement describing his own novels while describing Hardy's, "which he has divorced from the passionate purpose that issued him out of the earth into being."[12] Human identity, in other words, is split between our conscious, individual purpose and the unconscious, biological purpose we also carry within us. Hence the importance of marriage in *The Rainbow* and of the theology of marriage in the *Study* as a way of reconciling our two purposes. Lawrence is more optimistic about marriage than Hardy, who mainly attacks the institution. The difference partly derives from their different experiences of marriage. But it may also derive from the fact that Hardy is still a social reformer, still out to free us from the bonds of established institutions, while Lawrence wants to restore values to a society disastrously free of them. The difference may be one reason why Hardy is ironic, while Lawrence is notably without irony.

Lawrence's optimism also derives from Hardy's post-Darwinian metaphysic about the inevitable evolution of human consciousness and even the consciousness of the Innate Will in nature. "The sexual act," says Lawrence in the *Study*, "is not for the depositing of the seed. It is for leaping off into the unknown,"[13] for serving evolution. The sense of beyondness is the criterion of good sexual relations in *The Rainbow* and the novels that follow.

There emerges from Lawrence's analysis of Hardy's people a new diagram of identity as a small, well-lit area surrounded by an increasingly dark penumbra of unconsciousness opening out to external, impersonal forces. This leads to a system of judgment which condemns the attempt to shut out the darkness and live imprisoned in the well-lit ego. Thus Lawrence's analysis of the idealistic Clym in *The Return of the Native*:

> Impotent to *be*, he must transform himself, and live in an abstraction, in a generalization, he must identify himself with the system. He must live as Man or Humanity, or as the Community, or as Society, or as Civilization.... He already showed that thought is a disease of the flesh, and indirectly bore evidence that ideal

physical beauty is incompatible with emotional development and a full recognition of the coil of things.

Clym, who showed that highly conscious modern people cannot be beautiful, shut out the penumbra of unconsciousness connecting him with the Heath. The fenced-out darkness can seem as demonic as the fenced-in ego: "Was it his blood, which rose dark and potent out of Egdon [Heath], which hampered and confined the deity [within him], or was it his mind, that house built of extraneous knowledge and guarded by his will, which formed the prison?"[14]

Ursula in *The Rainbow* arrives at a similar diagram of her identity:

This lighted area, lit up by man's completest consciousness, she thought was all the world: that here all was disclosed for ever. Yet all the time, within the darkness she had been aware of points of light, like the eyes of wild beasts, gleaming, penetrating, vanishing. And her soul had acknowledged in a great heave of terror only the outer darkness.[15]

She succumbs to the darkness because she has had only momentary, ego-centered intuitions of it as fenced-out; hence the wild beasts who are menacing when repressed. But Ursula advances beyond Clym because she learns to reconcile consciousness with unconsciousness.

In assimilating Clym to *The Rainbow*, Lawrence is not misreading. His analysis of Clym is brilliantly valid. The sign of this is that Clym, with his lofty intellectual ambitions, studies so hard that he becomes blind and his blindness leads him back to the Heath—he finds contentment as a lowly furze cutter. Clym's salutary blindness, though Lawrence does not discuss it, may have given Lawrence the idea for his short story "The Blind Man," in which Maurice Pervin's blindness restores "the almost incomprehensible peace of immediate contact in darkness."[16] Pervin's blindness improves his marriage; whereas Clym's destroys his marriage, because Clym alternates between consciousness and unconsciousness while his wife Eustacia insists on his having both—his consciousness for worldly prestige, his unconsciousness presumably for sex. Clym's blindness seems to symbolize a decline in sexuality—a point Lawrence surprisingly ignores.

According to Lawrence's analysis, the two human purposes—individual and biological—determine the structure and imagery of Hardy's novels as well as his characterizations. There exists in Hardy's novels, writes Lawrence,

> a great background, vital and vivid, which matters more than the people who move upon it. . . . The vast unexplored morality of life itself, what we call the immorality of nature, surrounds us in its eternal incomprehensibility, and in its midst goes on the little human morality play, with its queer frame of morality and its mechanized movement; seriously, portentously, till some one of the protagonists chances to look out of the charmed circle, weary of the stage, to look into the wilderness raging round. Then he is lost, his little drama falls to pieces, or becomes mere repetition, but the stupendous theatre outside goes on enacting its own incomprehensible drama, untouched.[17]

The characters' two purposes parallel the two areas where the action takes place—the small, well-lit circle of human morality and the constantly encroaching amoral wilderness around it. (In traditional literature, instead, the human moral scheme pervades the universe.) Hardy's men—like Clym and Angel Clare, on the side of goodness, and Alec d'Urberville on the side of badness—alternate between the two areas. Hardy's tragic figures—usually women, like Eustacia and Tess; Jude is the exceptional male—inhabit both areas and are torn apart by the conflict. A sign of the tragic conflict is *Tess*'s earliest manuscript title: *The Body and Soul of Sue* (Tess's original name).[18]

Lawrence, I think, derives his metaphysic in the *Study* from the conflict he discerned in Hardy between conscious and unconscious principles. Since Hardy's heroes are mainly weighted on the side of consciousness and his heroines on the side of unconsciousness, it follows that Lawrence in his metaphysic (confirming in this contrast cultural prejudice) calls the conscious principle *male* and the unconscious *female*, while acknowledging that each person, and indeed each historical epoch, combines a different mixture of male and female principles. The men in Hardy who are in touch with unconscious forces of sexuality are mainly villains—like Alec in *Tess* and Troy in *Far from the Madding Crowd* (Arabella in *Jude the Obscure* is the exceptional woman in this group)—because they are seducers: they exploit sexuality. Lawrence, as we might expect, is more favorable to these sexually charged characters than most readers up to his time had been. But when Hardy ventures to say of Angel in *Tess*, who displays the Victorian virtues of chastity and strict moral judgment, that "with more animalism [Angel] would have been the nobler man," [19] Hardy is on the way to becoming Lawrence.

The great achievement of Lawrence's dialectical system in the *Study* is the recognition of the female principle as a positive force, equal if not superior in vitality to the male principle. When women in traditional literature are strong, they tend to be evil—like Lady Macbeth or Thackeray's Becky Sharp in *Vanity Fair*. The intelligence and strength of will of Lawrence's mother, as portrayed in *Sons and Lovers*, is on the whole damaging. Lawrence's recognition of a healthy female vitality must have come from his long tussle with his wife Frieda, a female powerhouse. But it derived also from Hardy's women who—beginning with the revolutionary character of the managerial Bathsheba in *Far from the Madding Crowd*—are usually more intelligent and stronger-willed than the men. The same can be said of the Brangwen women in *The Rainbow* and *Women in Love* (only Birkin is a match for them). The theme of many Hardy novels is the superior woman's problem in finding a suitable mate—a theme Hardy took from George Eliot, from Dorothea's problem in *Middlemarch*. When Lawrence writes that the germ of his early draft, *The Sisters*, was "woman becoming individual, self-responsible, taking her own initiative," [20] he is continuing the theme of George Eliot and Hardy with additions to Hardy's increase of sexual ramifications.

The month before Lawrence announced his projected book on Hardy's people, he wrote in the well-known "carbon" identity letter of 5 June 1914 a description of the new impersonal identity to be found in *The Rainbow*. Although the "carbon" identity letter precedes the letter proposing the *Study*, we have to remember that when Lawrence wrote the "carbon" identity letter he was about to *re*read Hardy and that what he had fundamentally learned had been learned from earlier readings and was already mainly incorporated in the novel he had just sent to Methuen. ("Have you ever read *Jude the Obscure?*" he asked Louie Burrows as early as 17 December 1910.) [21] The near coincidence of the "carbon" identity letter with the 15 July letter announcing his plan to write on Hardy's people suggests Lawrence's feeling that the new sense of identity in *The Rainbow* derived from Hardy and his consequent need to retrace his steps as a way of understanding what he had accomplished. The *Study of Hardy* confirms and systematizes the "carbon" identity letter.

"You mustn't look in my novel," Lawrence writes in this letter, "for the old stable *ego* of the character. There is another *ego* according to whose action the individual is unrecognizable." This other ego is the unconscious, impersonal element, the "carbon" identity. "My theme is carbon," writes Lawrence. "That which is physic—non-human, in humanity, is more interesting to me than the old-fashioned human element—which causes one to conceive a character in a certain moral scheme and make him consistent."[22]

In the *Study*, Lawrence says much the same thing when he points out the inconsistency of Hardy's characters:

> Nowhere, except perhaps in Jude, is there the slightest development of personal action in the characters: it is all explosive. . . . The rest explode out of the convention. They are people each with a real, vital, potential self . . . and this self suddenly bursts the shell of manner and convention and commonplace opinion, and acts independently, absurdly; without mental knowledge or acquiescence. And from such an outburst the tragedy usually develops. For there does exist, after all, the great self-preservation scheme [society], and in it we must all live.[23]

In the "carbon" identity letter and the *Study*, Lawrence is saying that he and Hardy treat their characters' social selves—the whole concern of the novel of manners—as the mere tip of the iceberg. The real action goes on underneath, rising to the surface sporadically in explosive or symbolic manifestations the logic and motives of which remain as mysterious to the characters as to the reader. In carrying the regression as far back as inanimate carbon, Lawrence goes a step further than Hardy, who roots his characters in vegetated landscape. Behind them both stands Wordsworth, who was the first to root his characters in landscape and to intensify their being through regression as far back as inanimate objects: the quality of the old leech-gatherer's existence, in "Resolution and Independence," is that of a huge stone that seems slightly, mysteriously animate. The innovation in Wordsworth, Hardy and Lawrence is the portrayal of characters as states of being rather than as defined by social class and moral choice—the criteria of traditional characterization. There remains, however, more social determination in Hardy than in Lawrence.

The paradigms of "carbon" identity and explosive characterization are especially apparent in *Women in Love*, which proceeds through a series of discontinuous stills or set scenes each designed to manifest the characters' unconscious or "carbon" identity. Gerald and Gudrun seal their sado-masochistic union in the scene on the island, where Gudrun defies the male principle by chasing away bullocks and finally by slapping Gerald across the face—a totally unexpected manifestation. Their relationship proceeds through arbitrary, unprepared-for scenes in which Gudrun swoons with masochistic excitement while Gerald torments his mare and subdues a huge hare, whose savage energy in whirling round as Gerald holds him by the ears suggests phallic power. Lawrence's use of animals to reveal to his characters their unconscious desires may derive from Hardy—from a scene like the sheep-shearing in *Far from the Madding Crowd*, in which Gabriel and Bathsheba discover their desire for each other through Gabriel's sexually suggestive way of handling a ewe while Bathsheba watches. Gabriel, we are told, dragged

> a frightened ewe to his shear-station, flinging it over upon its back with a dexterous twist of the arm. He lopped off the tresses about its head, and opened up the neck and collar, his mistress quietly looking on. "She blushes at the insult," murmured Bathsheba, watching the pink flush which arose and overspread the neck and shoulders of the ewe where they were left bare by the clicking of the shears.... Poor Gabriel's soul was fed with a luxury of content by having her over him.[24]

Similarly, in *Sons and Lovers*, Paul's sexually suggestive cherry-pelting of Miriam before their first intercourse may derive from Alec d'Urberville's sexually suggestive way of feeding Tess strawberries on their first meeting: "Tess eating in a half-pleased, half-reluctant state what d'Urberville offered her.... She obeyed like one in a dream"[25] (this is the pattern of her later rape–seduction by Alec). *The Rainbow*'s spectacular dance under moonlight, which releases the erotic unconscious of Ursula and Skrebensky, echoes the scene in *The Return of the Native* where Eustacia, temporarily fleeing her unhappy marriage to attend a village dance, meets there by Hardyan coincidence (as the fulfillment of her unconscious desire) her former lover Wildeve, who is also unhappily married. Their dance under moonlight provides erotic release: "These two [were] riding upon the whirlwind. The dance had come like an irresistible attack upon whatever sense of social order there was in their minds."[26]

The analysis of Hardy's explosive characterizations is Lawrence's most illuminating insight into Hardy's novels. It accounts for Bathsheba's sudden entanglement with Sergeant Troy, which runs counter to the sequence of events and Bathsheba's conscious intentions. Troy is a complete stranger to her when his spur becomes entangled in her dress one night in her garden. The crude bodily contact, which excites Bathsheba because of its outrageousness ("'she blushes at the insult,'" she had said of the "undressed" ewe), leads to the sealing of their union in the wildly explosive sword exercise scene, which with its phallic and sado-masochistic symbolism reveals to Bathsheba a stratum of sexual desire she knows nothing about. As Troy makes his sword cuts within a hair's breadth of her body, she feels penetrated: " 'Have you run me through?' " The experience becomes psychologically a kind of intercourse: "She felt powerless to withstand or deny him. . . . She felt like one who has sinned a great sin." This last in response to what turns out to have been a mere kiss. Because of its sexual archetypes—the phallic performance takes place in a vaginal or womblike "hollow amid the ferns"[27]—the sword exercise scene is the most Lawrencean scene in Hardy, though we probably have to have read Lawrence or Freud to appreciate the blatancy of its symbolism.

Bathsheba, the masterful woman who expresses her sexual interest in Gabriel Oak by tormenting him, gets a sexual thrill out of being brutally subdued by Sergeant Troy. Hardy's understanding of sado-masochism points toward Lawrence whom Yeats wrongly credited with having discovered the cruelty of love. Tess's relation with Alec d'Urberville is also sado-masochistic. Alec subdues her at the outset by driving her at terrifying speed to the d'Urberville mansion where she will be a servant. Then he "gave her the kiss of mastery." The master–servant relation enhances sado-masochism. Gabriel is Bathsheba's servant; Troy is her servant's lover. When Alec in the end insists that Tess return to him, she (in a scene pointing toward the scene in which Lawrence's Gudrun strikes Gerald) slaps him across the mouth with her heavy glove, drawing blood.

> "Now, punish me!" she said, turning up her eyes to him with the hopeless defiance of the sparrow's gaze before its captor twists its neck. "Whip me, crush me. . . . I shall not cry out. Once victim, always victim—that's the law!"

Alec in replying fills the role required of him: "'I was your master once! I will be your master again.' "[28] Tess returns to him.

Lawrence's analysis of Hardy's explosive characterizations accounts for the ambiguities of Tess's behavior at crucial moments of her life. Why does Tess take the job at the d'Urbervilles when it is clear from the start that Alec will be a danger to her? Why, after all her determined resistance to him, does Tess, on that most crucial night of her life, suddenly leap behind him on his horse and allow herself to be carried into the dark wood where she falls asleep so willingly that it remains impossible to determine whether she is then raped or seduced? (Did Lawrence learn from this scene how to portray Gerald's rapelike way of taking Gudrun the first time when, with the mud from his father's grave on his boots, he steals like a criminal into her family's house and breaks into her bedroom determined to have her?) Why cannot Tess, despite her good intentions, bring herself to tell Angel before their marriage about her relations with Alec? Angel might not then have felt betrayed by the confession which came too late. When Tess learns that Angel never saw the confessional letter she slipped under his door because the letter slipped under a rug, she lets this accident make the decision for her not to confess. According to the Victorian reading, the accident is a typically contrived Hardy coincidence. If we take a deep psychological view of the incident, however, it exemplifies an advanced technique for making an external event confirm an unconscious desire—Tess's desire to let nothing impede her marriage to Angel.

Why does Tess go back to Alec? And why, after Angel's reappearance, does Tess murder Alec when all she has to do is leave him? And why, finally, does Tess show so little interest in escaping with Angel after the murder? Why in the end does she lay herself down, almost willingly, as a human sacrifice on the altar at Stonehenge to be captured and executed?

Hardy's explanations are in the deep psychological manner overdetermined—which is to say that they are all partly valid, yet not one of them is the complete explanation. The reason Tess takes the job at the d'Urbervilles is to help her family financially; and that is one reason she goes back to Alec, though the reason is less satisfactory than before as a complete explanation. The night of the rape-seduction, she leaps on to Alec's horse in order to avoid a fight with his former mistress; but she also triumphs over the other girl by leaping on to the horse in front of her. Hardy suggests an even deeper reason when he says that Tess "abandoned herself to her impulse . . . and scrambled into the saddle behind him." Her unconscious acquiescence is confirmed by her falling asleep and by Hardy's further explanation that Tess was still a child with a woman's body. Another recurrent explanation is that Tess is the victim of a malignant fate—her mishaps are presented as ironies of fate.

Tess's problem throughout is her combination of strong conscience with strong sexual desire. She has one foot in what Lawrence calls Hardy's "human morality play," and the other in the swirl of the amoral biological force that joins our life to the cosmos. It is partly conscience, guilt over the ruin she feels she brought to her family's meager fortune, that impels her toward Alec. Instead of feeling rage over Angel's abandonment of her, she takes the blame upon herself and goes to work on the brutal Flintcomb-Ash Farm, with its infernal landscape, as a kind of penance. Most of Tess's misery is created by her conscience; for she condemns herself more strongly than does anyone else.

Equally strong is Tess's unconscious desire for a biological fulfillment leading through sexuality to death. Like Gabriel Oak in *Far from the Madding Crowd*, Tess falls asleep at crucial moments that, with her conscious acquiescence, advance her destiny. Here is Hardy's description of the conflict in Tess between conscience and biological destiny. She has just left Angel after promising to answer his proposal of marriage in a few days and at the same time tell him about her past.

> Tess flung herself down upon the rustling undergrowth of speargrass, as upon a bed, and remained crouching in palpitating misery broken by momentary shoots of joy, which her fears about the ending could not altogether suppress. In reality, she was drifting into acquiescence. Every see-saw of her breath, every wave of her blood, every pulse singing in her ears, was a voice that joined with nature in revolt against her scrupulousness. . . .In almost a terror of ecstasy Tess divined that, despite her many months of lonely self-chastisement, wrestlings, communings, schemes to lead a future of austere isolation, love's counsel would prevail.[29]

Similarly Clym, while waiting for Eustacia, often flings himself down amid vegetation as if to draw erotic strength from nature. Lawrence's Birkin in *Women in Love* flings himself down so, after Hermione has tried to kill him, as if to draw restorative strength from nature. Hardy's deep explanation as to why Tess finally consents to marry Angel without having confessed looks back to Wordsworth and forward to Lawrence: "The 'appetite for joy' [a Wordsworthian phrase] which pervades all creation, that tremendous force which sways humanity to its purpose, as the tide sways the helpless weed, was not to be controlled by vague lucubrations over the social rubric."[30]

The same biological drive leads Tess to seek death as well. She expresses throughout her longing for death. Her murder of Alec is a way of bringing on her own death; but it is also a fulfillment of their murderous sexual relation, a relation like that of Gerald and Gudrun. Gudrun's words to Gerald after she has slapped him across the face would apply to Tess after she slaps Alec. " 'You have struck the first blow,' " says Gerald. " 'And I shall strike the last,' " Gudrun replies.[31] After the murder Tess tells Angel: "I have killed him! . . . I feared long ago, when I struck him on the mouth with my glove, that I might do it some day.' "[32]

There has emerged since Lawrence's time two ways of reading *Tess* and Hardy's other major novels—the Victorian or moralistic way and the Lawrencean or deep psychological way. According to the moralistic reading, Tess is entirely Alec's victim—she entertains no sexual feeling for him.[33] She goes to him only to help her family; their first intercourse is a rape; she murders him to avenge the harm he has done her. The novel is largely a reformist attack on the double standard of sexual morality. According to the moralistic reading a malignant fate is the prime mover of events, while in the *Study* fate is hardly mentioned. We need to combine both readings, but it is the deep psychological reading that reveals the full measure of Hardy's greatness and accounts for what have seemed flaws in his characterization and plotting. Through our reading of Lawrence, both in the *Study* and the novels, we have come to understand that Hardy is important in the history of the English novel because he is the first to elaborate the sphere of unconscious motivation. Sterne alludes to the unconscious; the Brontës show intuitive flashes into it; Dickens, we now realize as the Victorians did not, symbolizes the unconscious through projections of it in the world of objects. But Hardy is the first English novelist to treat the unconscious analytically and to organize characterization and plot for the purpose of revealing the unconscious.

\*

In *Jude the Obscure,* Sue Bridehead is the best example of Hardy's explosive characterization. Sue's crucial decisions are never prepared for; it requires the deepest psychology to understand them, and many remain unfathomable. Why does she marry Phillotson, and even more puzzling why does she entirely on her own initiative return to him (repeating the pattern of Tess's return to Alec) when she is still in love with Jude to whom she has borne children? The usual answer is that she wants to do penance for having lived in sin with Jude, but the return of her repressed Christian conscience masks deeper motives.

Why, in the chain of events leading to the children's deaths, does Sue tell the landlady that she and Jude are not married? (This is a shock also for the reader, since the last we heard they went to London to be married.) Sue's unnecessary confession leads to the family's eviction from the only lodging they could find. The eviction and the refusal of other lodgings make a terrible impression on the oldest boy, who concludes: " 'It would be better to be out o' the world that in it, wouldn't it?' " Instead of comforting him, Sue agrees:

"It would almost, dear."
" 'Tis because of us children, too, isn't it, that you can't get a good lodging?"
"Well—people do object to children sometimes."
"Then if children make too much trouble, why do people have 'em?"
"O—because it is a law of nature." . . .
"I wish I hadn't been born!"
"You couldn't help it, my dear."
"I think that whenever children be born that are not wanted they should be killed directly, before their souls come to 'em."

Instead of assuring the boy of their love, Sue "did not reply." And she unnecessarily volunteers the information that there will be another baby. The boy responds with such horror—" 'O God, mother, you've never a-sent for another; and such trouble with what you've got!' "—as to indicate that this last piece of information makes him hang the other children and himself.

Hardy, in his usual way of offering an inadequate explanation in order to suggest others, begins this episode by saying that "Sue had not the art of prevarication." Would it have been a lie to tell the boy she loved him and to have withheld the information about the new baby? For all her beauty, intelligence and idealism, Sue emerges as a charming monster because she lacks instincts.

After the children's deaths, Sue realizes that "her discourse with the boy had been the main cause of the tragedy." She explains to Jude:

> I talked to the child as one should only talk to people of mature age.... I wanted to be truthful. I couldn't bear deceiving him as to the facts of life. And yet I wasn't truthful, for with a false delicacy I told him too obscurely.... Why didn't I tell him pleasant truths, instead of half-realities? ... I could neither conceal things nor reveal them![34]

The things she concealed were the facts of sex, thus making her explanation even more terrifying to the boy. Sue's fear of sex is always the deeper motive beneath her apparent ones. Yet she subscribes—showing Hardy's analysis here and elsewhere of a self-deceiving idealism—to an abstract ideal of free sex.

Lawrence brilliantly tells us that Jude and Sue do not feel that, in living together without marriage, they have sinned against Christianity or the community but that they have lied to themselves. "They knew it was no marriage; they knew it was wrong, all along they knew they were sinning against life, in forcing a physical marriage between themselves." Their uneasiness makes them seem more illicit to others than do ordinary illicit lovers. Theirs was no marriage because Sue was no woman. It was wrong of Jude to have forced sex upon her, and wrong of her to have borne children in order to make a false show of being a woman. Because their marriage had no consummation in the interchange of male and female principles, "they were," says Lawrence in a poetic passage showing his deep response to the novel, "too unsubstantial, too thin and evanescent in substance, as if the other solid pople might jostle right through them, two wandering shades as they were": Dantesque shades.

Lawrence again reveals motives deeper than the ostensible Christian ones in explaining Sue's return to Phillotson after the children's deaths:

> Then Sue ceases to be.... The last act of her intellect was the utter renunciation of her mind and the embracing of utter orthodoxy, where every belief, every thought, every decision was

made ready for her, so that she did not exist self-responsible. And then her loathed body . . . that too should be scourged out of existence. She chose the bitterest penalty in going back to Phillotson. . . . All that remained of her was the will by which she annihilated herself. That remained fixed, a locked centre of self-hatred, life-hatred so utter that it had no hope of death.³⁵

This sounds like a Lawrence novel. The last three sentences could be describing Gudrun, who chose the bitterest penalty in giving herself up to Loerke. Yet the analysis applies illuminatingly to Sue. Jude and Gerald, who have emotions, are granted the relief of death; Sue and Gudrun, who live entirely in the head, are not granted oblivion.

Lawrence's most important insight into *Jude the Obscure* is the statement that "Jude is only Tess turned round about. . . .Arabella is Alec d'Urberville, Sue is Angel Clare."³⁶ Since Lawrence says that both Tess and Jude contain within themselves the conflict between female sensuality and male intellect, one wonders why he goes on to speak of Jude as though he lived entirely in the head like Sue. Jude like Tess is strong in sexuality and conscience; that is why Jude succumbs to Arabella as Tess succumbs to Alec. The difference is that Jude is not on such friendly terms as Tess with his unconscious; unlike Tess, he does not fall asleep at crucial moments.

Jude and Sue—even more than Jude—are alienated from their unconscious. That is what makes them Hardy's first distinctively twentieth-century characters. Angel's repression of his unconscious is still Victorian in that it can be explained by lingering religiousness, as Jude's and Sue's cannot. Hardy's remark that Tess expresses "the ache of modernism"³⁷ does not gibe with the rest of her character; but the phrase suits Jude and Sue, who appeared only four years later (*Tess*, 1891; *Jude*, 1895). It requires Lawrence's metaphysic—in which he traces the cultural evolution of the West from female communal Judaism to male individualistic Protestantism—to account for the astounding fact, finally stated in the *Study*'s penultimate chapter, that the male principle should have come to reside in a certain kind of modern woman. "Sue," says Lawrence, "is scarcely a woman at all, though she is feminine enough. . . .One of the supremest products of our civilization is Sue, and a product that well frightens us."³⁸

*Tess* and *Jude* are the two Hardy novels Lawrence discusses in detail. We can see why since they are the two that treat sex most explicitly, making a bridge to Lawrence's own work. The chapter on

*Jude* is the *Study*'s climax, and in this chapter the discussion of Sue makes the most important bridge to Lawrence's work. For it is in the character of Sue, as Lawrence analyzes her, that Hardy makes the definitive break with the Victorian novel, in which the problem was to arrive at the point of sexuality by finding the right mate while staying within the laws of God and society. With Sue sexuality itself becomes the problem, even a problem in pathology. From Sue on, we encounter characters (especially in Lawrence) who do not want sex or want it perversely. The connection in Sue of idealism with sexual deficiency points toward Miriam in Lawrence's *Sons and Lovers*. Paul Morel's choice in that novel between Miriam and Clara resembles Jude's choice between Sue and Arabella, with the difference that Paul has his own problem in his Oedipal attachment to his mother. Lawrence reads more sexual problems into Jude (perhaps because he identifies himself with him) than most readers would find.

With Sue, as Lawrence points out, Hardy makes a first attack on the cult of virginity, on all those novelistic virgins who have been held up as eminently desirable for marriage. With Sue, Hardy shows how virginity can become a pathological state of mind. Sue remains psychologically a virgin (her name Bridehead means *maidenhead* or virginity) even after she has slept with Jude and Phillotson and given birth to Jude's children. We can read back from Hardy's explicit treatment of sexual deficiency in Sue to find hints that the idealism of earlier characters like Angel and Clym may be linked with sexual deficiency. We can also read back from *Sons and Lovers* to find an Oedipal attachment between Clym and his mother, who sounds like Mrs Morel in opposing Clym's marriage.

So far Lawrence goes along with Hardy, explaining what he considers to be Hardy's conscious intentions. Lawrence breaks with Hardy over the issue of the sexually potent characters whom Lawrence calls "aristocrats," and the issue of society's role in the novels. On these issues Lawrence apparently feels he is fulfilling Hardy's unconscious intentions.

Hardy, we are told, has the predilection of all artists for the aristocrat, because "the aristocrat alone has occupied a position where he could afford to *be*, to be himself." But Hardy also shares the bourgeois moral antagonism to the aristocrat, making his aristocrats die or making "every exceptional person a villain."[39] Lawrence seems to have derived from Hardy his romantic notion of aristocracy as signifying existential potency rather than social class. Hardy likes to give his existentially potent characters vaguely aristocratic or pseudo-aristocratic connections—Tess, Alec, Troy, Eustacia are the best known examples; Fitzpiers in *The Woodlanders* is another. Through the three versions of *Lady Chatterley's Lover*, Lawrence keeps refining the gamekeeper in order to show that he, rather than Sir Clifford Chatterley, is the true aristocrat.

Hardy's fault, says Lawrence, is that he always stands "with the community in condemnation of the aristocrat," when "his private sympathy is always with the individual against the community." Hardy gives to his distinct individualities—characters like Troy, Clym, Tess and Jude (Lawrence should have added Sue)—"a weak life-flow, so that they cannot break away from the old adhesion" to the communal morality. Tess, for example, "sided with the community's condemnation of her." Tess does, as I have suggested, internalize a social condemnation harsher than anything objectively apparent until her execution, which is itself curiously muted.

"Hardy is a bad artist," says Lawrence, "because he must condemn Alec d'Urberville, according to his own personal creed." But Alec is "a rare man who seeks and seeks among women for one of such character and intrinsic female being as Tess." Similarly Arabella's distinction is that she chooses "a sensitive, deep-feeling man" like Jude, which no "coarse, shallow woman" would do. "Arabella was, under all her disguise of pig-fat and false hair, and vulgar speech, in character somewhat an aristocrat. She was, like Eustacia, amazingly lawless, even splendidly so. She believed in herself and she was not altered by any outside opinion of herself." It is surprising to see Arabella labelled an aristocrat and Sue a bourgeois when Arabella is the conventional one who skillfully conceals her misdemeanors and manages to marry the two men she sleeps with.

Alec and Troy, we are told, "could reach some of the real sources of the female in a woman, and draw from them. . . . And, as a woman instinctively knows, such men are rare. Therefore they have a power over a woman. They draw from the depth of her being. And what they draw, they betray." The same applies to Arabella. These sensualists betray the depths they draw on because they are exploitive in love—they gratify themselves without giving back the male or female principles that would create an interchange. They dominate the relation because they are unwilling to submit to the development in themselves required for the male–female interchange that yields full consummation. "Jude, like Tess, wanted full consummation. Arabella, like Alec . . . resisted full consummation."[40] It is a sign of their inability to develop that both Arabella and Alec go through a period of evangelical conversion that leaves no final effect upon them. In *Women in Love*, Lawrence uses as a criterion of approval the capacity for development: Ursula and Birkin are the only characters with this capacity. Lawrence—whose aim is to reconcile the conflicts that Hardy leaves unreconciled—works out a way of achieving full consummation through what he calls "star-equilibrium," a metaphor he may have taken from Hardy's description of Clym's and Eustacia's harmonious first months of marriage: "They were like those double stars which revolve round and round each other, and from a distance appear to be one."[41]

Lawrence criticizes Hardy for coming down, in the conflict between the individual and society, on the side of society when social judgments no longer express God's judgment but are merely relative. "Eustacia, Tess or Sue," says Lawrence, "were not at war with God, only with Society. Yet they were all cowed by the mere judgment of man upon them, and all the while by their own souls they were right. . . . Which is the weakness of modern tragedy, where transgression against the social code is made to bring destruction, as though the social code worked our irrevocable fate."[42] Actually Hardy agrees, more than Lawrence realizes, about the relativity of social judgment. I have already quoted the passage in which he says that Tess's desire for Angel "was not to be controlled by vague lucubrations over the social rubric." Tess feels ashamed of having suffered over mere conscience, when she beholds nature's cruelty in the suffering of pheasants left wounded by hunters. Wringing the pheasants' necks to end their pain, "she was ashamed of herself for her gloom of the night, based on nothing more tangible than a sense of condemnation under an arbitrary law of society which had no foundation in Nature."[43] The injustice of society is attacked throughout *Jude*.

What surprises Lawrence is that Hardy portrays a world where society still sends out signals strong enough, even if of doubtful validity, to torment his characters. In Lawrence's novels, by the time of *Women in Love* (1920), such signals have ceased: social proprieties are no longer an obstacle to anyone's desires. Lawrence portrays a world that has become increasingly apparent since World War I. In their treatment of society, the difference between Hardy and Lawrence is one of historical situation. Hardy's historical situation is better for the novel than Lawrence's, since the novel's original subject is the hero's exploration of and conflict with social reality. For such a subject the novelist requires a society complex enough to be worth exploring and powerful enough to be a worthy antagonist. Because such a society has largely disappeared by the time of *Women in Love* (1920), Lawrence evolves there and later a genre—the first signs of which are the ritualized scenes in *The Rainbow* (1915)—that substitutes for social notation the externalization of internal states of being: this genre exists on the borderline between myth and novel.

Already in Hardy's novels, where society still pretends to an authority it has lost, we find the beginnings of a transition to the mythical mode. The transition can be detected in Hardy's habit of presenting characters first as distantly perceived figures barely separable from the landscape before they approach and take on the lineaments of individuals. The transition can also be detected in Hardy's much criticized use of coincidences and other "clumsy" narrative devices, all of which sacrifice verisimilitude to set up highly concentrated scenes that permit the explosive revelation of internal states of being. Hardy's coincidences point toward Lawrence's Freudian dictum that there are no accidents, for Hardy's coincidences allow his characters to fulfill their desires and destinies. Hardy's irony derives first from the fact there still is a society worth attacking ironically, and second from the fact that what appears to be chance turns out to be design—that of fate and/or the characters' unconscious.

In the "Moony" chapter of *Women in Love*, Lawrence uses a Hardyan coincidence and accounts for it psychologically. Ursula is walking by a lake in moonlight at a time when Birkin is abroad. "She wished for something else out of the night." Soon "she saw a shadow moving by the water. It would be Birkin," she thinks before recognizing him. "He had come back then, unawares." That last word is ambiguous; it is the adverb Wordsworth uses with equal ambiguity when the narrator of "Resolution and Independence" suddenly beholds the leech-gatherer standing by a pool: "I saw a Man before me unawares." In Lawrence "unawares" seems to mean that Birkin has returned without telling her, in response to her desire, also that he is unaware of being observed. Ursula justifies spying on him by thinking: "How can there be any secrets, we are all the same organisms? How can there be any secrecy, when everything is known to all of us?"[44] Hardy's coincidences can be justified by the possibility that all the characters share one mind. The possibility dissolves the distinction between fate and the characters' individual unconsciousness.

In the *Study of Hardy*, Lawrence rewrites Hardy's novels and criticizes his deficiencies in such a way as to arrive at his own novels by an unbroken continuum. The *Study* is important as criticism just because it tells us as much about Lawrence as about Hardy to the enlargement of both writers' stature. When we think of all Hardy managed to say under the restrictions laid down by readers and editors even more prudish than the ones who harassed Lawrence, we can only conclude from what Lawrence shows us in the *Study* that Hardy, with his sensitivity to historical change, would, had he been born a generation later, have become a novelist very much like D. H. Lawrence.

This essay was first published in *The Thomas Hardy Annual*, No. 3 (Macmillan, 1985).

CHAPTER SIX

# Whitman and the Poetics of Lawrence

ROBERTS W. FRENCH

I

Walt Whitman remained a major influence throughout Lawrence's life. At every point he was a force to contend with, a spirit to be placated or driven away; he could not be lightly dismissed or ignored. On those occasions when Lawrence found him unsatisfactory and rejected him, the frequently abusive language indicated the depth of the attachment; Whitman had to be repelled with the strongest weapons available, for nothing less would have sufficed. Lawrence had somehow to go *beyond* Whitman, to establish his own position, and that was difficult, as the two had much in common. Thus, whether he was breaking away from Whitman or following, Lawrence acted with passion; what he could not do was be indifferent. The range of his attitudes may be conveniently seen in the third and final version of his essay on Whitman, which moves with startling suddenness from sneering vituperation to heartfelt praise.

At first the influence of Whitman is not readily apparent, for Lawrence's early poems, rhymed and stanzaic in form, find their models in Hardy, pre-eminently, and in the great Victorians, including Browning and Meredith. It is not until the publication of *Look! We Have Come Through!*, when Lawrence was thirty-two, that Whitman appears clearly visible as a major force behind the poetry. His presence, however, had long been felt in other ways; for Whitman's part in the development of D. H. Lawrence was more basic than the influence of literary techniques and mannerisms (although these were of great importance), and more essential. From the beginning Whitman gave Lawrence a sense of artistic freedom and integrity; he showed directions in which it was possible to move. Large areas of thought and feeling were available to Lawrence because Whitman had been there first, the territory was spacious, though little known. As Lawrence generously acknowledged, Whitman was the great explorer: "Whitman, the one man breaking a way ahead. Whitman, the one pioneer. And only Whitman. . . . Ahead of Whitman nothing. Ahead of all poets, pioneering into the wilderness of unopened life, Whitman. Beyond him, none."[1] Whitman showed how one could pass through boundaries, through conventions of thought and feeling, to new discoveries. He extended the limits. It is fitting that the *Look!* volume, the one in which Whitman first appeared as a distinct controlling force, was also the one in which Lawrence discovered and, in effect, declared his poetic originality; somewhat paradoxically, Whitman's influence led him to independence. Whitman would have understood and approved:

> I am the teacher of athletes,
> He that by me spreads a wider breast than my own proves the width of my own,
> He most honors my style who learns under it to destroy the teacher.[2]

What Whitman gave Lawrence, finally, was the example of a state of mind: adventurous, unashamed, tenacious, relentless in its pursuits, firm in its convictions, unmoved by the demands of popular taste, and above all true to the forces that compelled it. Prime among these forces was a vision of human potential shared, in certain essential respects, by both Whitman and Lawrence; for both were driven and inspired, in their different ways, by the insistent need to show humanity what it could be. The role is that of the prophet. A prophet has, above all, a commanding sense of human possibility; he may say, with Blake, "If the doors of perception were cleansed every thing would appear to man as it is, infinite. / For man has closed himself up, till he sees all things thro' narrow chinks of his cavern."[3] The prophet demands nothing less than a change in human apprehension; and the change must be total, "radical" in the most basic sense: at the roots. As Lawrence wrote in his note to "The Crown": "It is no use trying merely to modify present forms. The whole great form of our era will have to go. And nothing will really send it down but the new shoots of life springing up and slowly bursting the foundations. And one can do nothing but fight tooth and nail to defend the new shoots of life from being crushed out, and let them grow. We can't make life. We can but fight for the life that grows in us."[4]

It is significant that a certain few of our poets—notably Blake, Whitman and Lawrence—are frequently spoken of as prophets, while others, no less impassioned or certain of their inspiration, are not: Milton, for example, or Shelley. The reasons may be many, but most central is the consideration that prophecy must come—or must *seem* to come—unlooked for; it cannot be acquired by human effort, and it is beyond the rational will. As unpredictable as the wind, it bloweth where it listeth; and its comings and goings resist analysis. About prophecy and the prophetic poets there must appear to be something miraculous, inexplicable. Milton and Shelley had the advantages of wealth and education, and they labored hard to make themselves into poets of the first rank; one is always conscious of the human effort involved. Blake, Whitman and Lawrence may have labored no less hard, but they appear to be more the products of spontaneous inspiration beyond their control than of education and training. Certainly nothing in their working-class backgrounds or family situations would suggest likely origins for major poets; if poets were to be made, rather than born, one would not go to Blake, Whitman or Lawrence for models of training as one might go to Milton or Shelley, with their superb classical educations and the abundant leisure time that wealth provided for them. Blake, Whitman and Lawrence were apparently *born* to be poets no matter what their beginnings or what forms their lives took. Like the prophets, they seemed compelled to speak as they were bidden, their words prompted by some force beyond human limitations.

The prophet's gift might well be called a curse, for prophets are doomed to failure. Possessed of a vision not shared by other men, they must speak of it relentlessly, with an extraordinary sense of urgency, for it is essential to their being that they try to bring others into the world of their perceptions. They are defined by their mission; and their mission inevitably fails, for the fact is that other men, not being prophets, cannot share the prophetic vision. To them, the prophet seems to be speaking of some other world: as indeed he is, with the difference that to the prophet this other world, the world of potential fulfilled, is the real one, while to ordinary men it appears to be illusion. All prophets from Moses onward have had to accommodate themselves to failure. Whitman knew, in his later years, that he had not achieved his goals, and all he could do was to look to the future for vindication; Lawrence knew the same, and his response was to retreat into moods of misanthropic scorn and isolation.

While Whitman labored to become the prophet of democracy, even proclaiming himself as such in reviews of his own work. Lawrence made no overt claims to being a prophet of any sort. And yet he could describe himself occasionally in prophetic terms—for example, in a letter of 1913 where he wrote: "I often think one ought to be able to pray, before one works—and then leave it to the Lord. . . . I always feel as if I stood naked for the fire of Almighty God to go through me—and it's rather an awful feeling."[5] God's spokesman: that is the prophet.

But whatever Lawrence's claims for himself—and he always felt that his business was not to make claims, but to write—it is clear that others were willing to claim much for him. Like Whitman in his later years, Lawrence strongly impressed others not so much by the power of his assertions as by the quality of awareness he demonstrated through every nuance of being; he might have said with Whitman, "I and mine do not convince by arguments, similes, rhymes, / We convince by our presence" (*LG*, p. 155). Following an afternoon spent with Lawrence in 1927, Aldous Huxley noted in his diary: "Of most other eminent people I have met I feel that at any rate I belong to the same species as they do. But this man has something different and superior in kind, not degree." Five years later Huxley confirmed his original impression: " 'Different and superior in kind.' I think almost everyone who knew him well must have felt that Lawrence was this. A being, somehow, of another order, more sensitive, more highly conscious, more capable of feeling than even the most gifted of common men. . . . He looked at things with the eyes, so it seemed, of a man who had been at the brink of death and to whom, as he emerges from the darkness, the world reveals itself as unfathomably beautiful and mysterious." Huxley quotes a mutual friend as saying of Lawrence, simply, "He sees more than a human being ought to see."[6] The prophet does indeed see more than others, and he is intent on communicating his vision: nothing is more important. If he were to succeed, human life would be transformed utterly, and the world would be born again.

As prophets, Whitman and Lawrence shared an essentially pragmatic concept of art and poetry. Poetry, they insisted in various ways, should influence human actions and sensibilities; the greatest poet is necessarily a teacher, and his deepest purpose has to do with the refinement of the human mind. "I say," wrote Whitman, "the profoundest service that poems or any other writings can do for their reader is not merely to satisfy the intellect, or supply something polish'd and interesting, nor even to depict great passions, or persons or events, but to fill him with vigorous and clean manliness, religiousness, and give him *good heart* as a radical possession and habit" (*LG*, p. 570). Lawrence was explicit about the intentions of art and—in the age of Joyce and Rilke and Proust—curiously anachronistic in his concepts, though not in his methods. "We judge a work of art," he wrote, "by its effect on our sincere and vital emotion, and nothing else."[7] If art, after all, does not somehow improve our sensibilities, of what use is it? The true artist, Lawrence wrote, "*always* substitutes a finer morality for a grosser" (*Phoenix*, p. 525); nevertheless, he detested moral schemes in literature, and he qualified his concept of morality in another essay published in the same year (1925) by saying: "If a novel reveals true and vivid relationships, it is a moral work, no matter what the relationships may consist in" (*Phoenix*, p. 530). Lawrence's ideas about morality created problems throughout his life; nevertheless, he insisted on the religious nature of his inspirations. In this respect he followed Whitman. "I claim everything for religion," Whitman said; "after the claims of my religion are satisfied nothing is left for anything else: yet I have been called irreligious—an infidel (God help me!): as if I could have written a word of the Leaves without its religious background."[8] Lawrence made similar claims: "primarily I am a passionately religious man," he wrote; and elsewhere he noted, with perhaps a touch of regret, "one has to be so terribly religious, to be an artist" (*CL*, 1. 273, 189). It is one of the great ironies of literary history that Whitman and Lawrence, both so deeply committed to religion and morality, were both denounced for immorality and sacrilege. As prophets they were thoroughly misunderstood. Neither Whitman nor Lawrence, of course, pretended to be religious in any conventional sense; what was sacred to them was, finally, existence itself, the mere being: life. Just to be alive was sufficient cause for celebration: "It seems to me that everything in the light and air ought to be happy, / Whoever is not in his coffin and the dark grave let him know he has enough" (*LG*, pp. 427–428). As Lawrence put it, "The only reason for living is being fully alive...."[9]

## II

To be fully alive means to live in the present: to commit oneself entirely to the passing moment. For both Whitman and Lawrence the concept of *immediacy* is central to their thought and their art. Whitman insists on it; the best has not been, nor is it yet to come. It is here, in the immediate present: "The minute that comes to me over the past decillions, / There is no better than it and now" (*LG*, p. 50). It was precisely this sense of immediacy, everywhere apparent in Whitman's poetry, that Lawrence particularly valued, for it brought art close to the most important concern, life itself in its constant flow and change. In his preface to the American edition of *New Poems* (1920), Lawrence observed that poetry "is, as a rule, either the voice of the far future, exquisite and ethereal, or it is the voice of the past, rich, magnificent." Such poetry, he continued, "must have that exquisite finality, perfection which belongs to all that is far off. It is in the realm of all that is perfect." Perfection might seem to be a desirable characteristic of art, but Lawrence's aesthetics tend otherwise. It is *life* that matters, and perfection is dead, subject neither to movement nor time. What Lawrence valued was "another kind of poetry: the poetry of that which is at hand: the immediate present. In the immediate present there is no perfection, nor consummation, nothing finished." It is this sort of poetry that reflects the nature of existence, its dynamic qualities of flux and motion, its surging energy: "Life, the ever-present, knows no finality, no finished crystallization. The perfect rose is only a running flame, emerging and flowing off, and never in any sense at rest, static, finished." Of the poetry of the present, the poetry of life, the best example, Lawrence insisted, was Whitman's; and he added, significantly: "The clue to all his utterance lies in the sheer appreciation of the instant moment, life surging itself into utterance at its very well-head" (*Phoenix*, pp. 218–220).

This sense of immediacy, of "life surging itself into utterance," formed the center of Lawrence's aesthetics. Anyone reading through Lawrence's works will encounter it at every turn, in one form or another. In his essay. "The Novel," for example, he listed three qualities essential to fiction; the first is, simply, that the novel must be "quick": alive. "Nothing is important but life," he had written in another essay (*Phoenix*, p. 534), and this passionate belief is a compelling force behind his prophecy. A good measure of Lawrence's prophetic fury may be explained by his urgent conviction that all men are confronted by one essential choice, life or death, and most choose wrong, or fail to see that there *is* a choice. Like the Old Testament prophets, Lawrence presented absolutes: either/or there can be nothing else; those not committed to affirmation are lost. "We have to choose," he wrote, "between the quick and the dead. The quick is God-flame, in everything. And the dead is dead" (*Phoenix II*, p. 419). The choice is simple, as it is in Deuteronomy, where God proclaims to the Israelites, "I have set before thee this day life and good, and death and evil . . . therefore choose life" (Duet. 30:15,19).

Quickness, life, is at the center, and Lawrence praised Whitman above all for his penetration into the essential vitality of human existence. "He is so near the quick," Lawrence noted with admiration (*Phoenix*, p. 220). Quickness was all. "The quick," Lawrence observed in the second revision of his Whitman essay, "is the living being, the quick of quicks is the individual soul. And it is here, at the quick, that Whitman proceeds to find the experience of infinitude, his vast extension, or concentrated intensification into Allness. He carries the conquest to its end."[10] If Whitman had made no other contribution to Lawrence's development than the promotion of this deep commitment to life, he would have done enough, for Lawrence would be unrecognizable without it.

The great failure, then, is the failure to *live*—fully, through the range of emotions and senses, intensely at every moment: to be, that is, fully human. And yet the failure is widespread, as the deepest impulses of human nature are constantly denied. The dominant force is that of repression; we fear to be ourselves. "We are *afraid* of the instincts," Lawrence wrote. "We are *afraid* of the intuition within us" (*Phoenix*, p. 556). He might have added, as he everywhere implied, we are afraid of our bodies, afraid of sex, afraid of human relationships, afraid of death. As writer and prophet he sought to eradicate the fear that prevents us from fully accepting our humanity. It is a mission much like that of Whitman, who would have us begin again by first accepting our physical being in a physical world:

> As Adam early in the morning,
> Walking forth from the bower refresh'd with sleep,
> Behold me where I pass, hear my voice, approach,

> Touch me, touch the palm of your hand to my body as I pass,
> Be not afraid of my body.                (*LG*, p.111)

The ferocity of Lawrence's attacks on humankind can in part be explained by his revulsion at seeing that given the choice between life and death, we choose death. As much as Eliot, Lawrence wrote about the living dead; in his poems as in his essays and novels, he pondered "the great tragedy of our material-mechanical civilization / crushing out the natural human life" (*CP*, p. 508). He asked, as Eliot might have asked, "What have they done to you, men of the masses, creeping back and forth to work?" (*CP*, p. 630). Human lives are mean, sneaking and contemptible when they could be so much more—when they could be almost godlike. "What's the good of a man," Lawrence wrote, "unless there's the glimpse of a god in him?" (*CP*, p. 671).

The theme is Whitman's, as it is also, of course, Emerson's and Thoreau's—two authors whom Lawrence was reading with great enthusiasm at the same time he was discovering Whitman.[11] All three American writers assert a splendor that is to be had for the imagining; but true apprehension is everywhere repressed. "Shams and delusions," Thoreau complained, "are esteemed for soundest truths, while reality is fabulous."[12] And as Emerson noted, with deep regret: "On the brink of the waters of life and truth, we are miserably dying."[13] The poets, Emerson insisted, are the liberating gods. They can change our visions and our minds; they can bring us to another world, the true one. Thus Whitman, responding to Emerson's demands for poetry, frequently made statements calculated to startle his readers into new perceptions. "*A child said What is the grass?*" Who can say? The child is wiser than the adult; just to ask the question indicates a superior apprehension. What *is* the grass? Nothing merely physical, for the possibilities of perception are infinite. The grass is many things, all dependent on the quality of the imagination that perceives it. Perhaps, Whitman suggested, it is "the flag of my disposition," or "the handkerchief of the Lord," or "itself a child," or "a uniform hieroglyphic," or "the beautiful uncut hair of graves" (*LG*, pp. 33–34). It is all these, and more; to dismiss it with some easy definition is to impose too limited a view on the nature of existence and create restrictions where there need be none. The poet does not know what the grass is; he knows only that it is grander and more mysterious than is generally thought. In his role as teacher Whitman insists first of all on reforming our perceptions so that we may begin again in a transformed world:

> Long enough have you dream'd contemptible dreams,
> Now I wash the gum from your eyes,
> You must habit yourself to the dazzle of the light and of every moment of your life. (*LG*, p.84)

Lawrence intended to do no less. In one of his most revealing comments on poetry he wrote: "The essential quality of poetry is that it makes a new effort of attention, and 'discovers' a new world within the known world" (*Phoenix*, p. 255). Lawrence's life and works are marked by a dominating intensity derived in large measure from this visionary compulsion, this insistence on penetrating through the appearances of the known world to the life within; his stance is, quite literally, that of the "seer," the prophet whose insight into the nature of things sets him apart from the people to whom he preaches. A sense of urgency brought about by the demands of a heightened awareness marked everything Lawrence did; as John Middleton Murry has commented: "At the end we know one thing and one thing alone: that Mr Lawrence believes, with all his heart and soul, that he is revealing to us the profound and naked reality of life, that it is a matter of life and death to him that he should persuade us it is a matter of life and death to ourselves to know that these things are so."[11]

### III

If it is "the new effort of attention," the act of discovery, that is the essential quality of poetry, certain aesthetic considerations must necessarily follow. Here again Lawrence follows the example of Whitman, to whom, it will be recalled, Lawrence gave extraordinary praise for his role as pioneer, explorer, discoverer. If the poet as prophet is engaged above all in the discovery of truth, the only form that matters is the one that permits him to be honest. He must claim to be somehow above literature and beyond art; for literary art is a contrivance, the product of manipulation and craft, inherently "rhetorical" and therefore deceitful, concerned with *effect*, not with the statement of truth. "I feel about literature," Whitman commented in his later years, "what Grant did about war. He hated war. I hate literature" (Traubel, 1.58). He later remarked, "The trouble with most poems is that they are nothing but poems—all poetry, all literary, not in any way human" (Traubel, 2. 144). "No one will get at my verses," he asserted, "who insists upon viewing them as a literary performance" (*LG*, p. 574).

Like Whitman, Lawrence disdained the effects of art. In an early letter (1908) he stated clearly what he wanted in poetry, and he never wavered in his demands. "Before everything," he wrote, "I like sincerity, and a quickening spontaneous emotion" (*CL*, 1. 21). The truth of feeling was primary; throughout his life Lawrence reacted with scorn and contempt for anything he took to be pretense or pose. His strongest rejection of Whitman, most notably, came about because Lawrence refused to believe that Whitman's claim of universal sympathy were sincere; nothing could convince him that Whitman meant what he said. It had to be fake—"All that false exuberance," Lawrence snorted (*SCAL*, p. 165). And in *More Pansies* Lawrence made his "Retort to Whitman," again denouncing what he took to be Whitman's fraudulent claims: "And whoever walks a mile full of false sympathy / walks to the funeral of the whole human race" (*CP*, p. 653).

First must come the revelation of truth; from this all else follows. One thing that follows, most basically, is the autobiographical nature of the poetry of both Lawrence and Whitman. The poem must be authentic, with emotions truly and accurately portrayed; and the poet, after all, knows no one so well as himself. It would hardly be credible to speak for humanity while ignoring the self. Like that early explorer, Montaigne, and like that much later one, Freud, Whitman and Lawrence both found that the great discoveries were to be made—*had* to be made—within the self; nowhere else could the poet speak with such authority. What Gay Wilson Allen has said of *Leaves of Grass* would apply just as well to Lawrence's *Complete Poems*: that it is "one of the most personal, and in many ways the most naively frank, collections of poetry ever written."[15] Whitman knew what he was doing. "I will not reject any subject," he said, "because the treatment is too personal. As my stuff settles into shape, I am told (and sometimes myself discover, uneasily, but feel all right about it in calmer moments) it is mainly autobiographic, and even egotistic after all—which I finally accept, and am contented so"

(*LG*, p. 770). When Lawrence sent the manuscript of *Amores* to Lady Ottoline Morrell in 1916, he said of the poems, "You see they make a sort of inner history of my life, from 20 to 26" (*CL*, l. 419); and in the preface to his *Collected Poems* (1928) he commented: "I have tried to establish a chronological order, because many of the poems are so personal that, in their fragmentary fashion, they make up a biography of an emotional and inner life" (*CP*, p. 27). The inner history of his life was to be Lawrence's constant subject; it is a record of continual search and discovery.

If the discovery of truth, of the new world within the known world, is the essential purpose of the poet, it follows that any suggestion of decoration or ornament in poetry is to be shunned; anything that would divert from the clear statement of truth must be ruthlessly excluded. Whitman's poetry may not always impress us as being free of rhetorical invention—much of it is highly mannered—but his intentions were to work toward clarity (indeed, many of the later poems may be criticized for being *too* clear: successful as statement, but insufficient as poetry). In an undated note Whitman indicated a guiding aesthetic principle: "In future *Leaves of Grass. Be more severe* with the final revision of the poem, nothing will do, not one word or sentence that is not *perfectly clear*—with positive purpose—harmony with the name, nature, drift of the poem. Also *no ornaments*, especially *no ornamental adjectives*, unless they have come molten hot, and imperiously prove themselves. *No ornamental similes at all—not one: perfect transparent clearness*, sanity, and health are wanted—*that* is the *divine style*—O if it can be attained—" (*LG*, p. 764). Poetry must be fully exposed, naked, with nothing to detract from the statement of truth. As a poetical principle, Whitman's determination to achieve *"perfect transparent clearness"* might well have served as a model for Lawrence, who expressed similar aims. "The essence of poetry," he wrote, "with us in this age of stark and unlovely actualities is a stark directness, without a shadow of a lie, or a shadow of deflection anywhere. Anything can go, but this stark, bare, rocky directness of statement, this alone makes poetry, today" (*CL*, 1. 413).

"Directness of statement": that must come first. "The only comfort," Lawrence wrote, "in the long run, is the truth, however bitter it be" (*CL*, 1. 370). In poetry, Lawrence came, after early and only partially successful attempts to write in stanzaic forms, to follow Whitman's pioneering experiments in free verse, for only free verse was sufficiently flexible to represent the movements of the mind in action. Rhymed and stanzaic forms were deceptive; completed, polished, contrived, they distorted truth for the sake of art. It was essential that poetry be—to return to Lawrence's favorite adjective—"quick": alive and moving, not finished and dead. Paradoxically, the best art had to be imperfect, for only in imperfection could there be the essential quickness. "The quick of all the universe," said Lawrence, "of all creation, is the incarnate carnal self. Poetry gave us the clue: free verse: Whitman. Now we know" (*CP*, p. 185). If poetry is an act of discovery, in particular of the discovery of the "incarnate carnal self," it is through free verse that the discovery is to be made. Free verse is verse that is free to move as the mind moves, flowing through changes of thought and feeling, always poised on the point of moving on; in free verse we look for, and find, "the insurgent naked throb of the instant moment" (*CP*, p. 185). Free verse is concerned with vitality, not with finalities; as it moves through fleeting, constantly shifting apprehensions, it comes closest to the dynamic forces of life, to the energy that moves all things, to the ways of God: "God is the great urge that has not yet found a body / but urges towards incarnation with the great creative urge" (*CP*, p. 691). Or, in Whitman's version, "Urge and urge and urge, / Always the procreant urge of the world" (*LG*, p. 31).

Both for Whitman and Lawrence it became important that poetry appear to be unfinished, in a state of process rather than presented as a product. Not only does the unfinished state convey life and energy; it also most fully engages the reader, stimulating life and energy in the mind. "I round and finish little, if anything," wrote Whitman, "and could not, consistently with my scheme. The reader will always have his or her part to do, just as much as I have had mine. I seek less to state or display any theme or thought, and more to bring you, reader, into the atmosphere of the theme or thought—there to pursue your own flight" (*LG*, p. 570). Whitman's concept is remarkably in advance of its time; its insistence on incompleteness, on the necessarily fragmented state of art and existence, will eventually reach fruition in such characteristically modern works as Eliot's *Waste Land*, Pound's *Cantos*, Williams' *Paterson*, Berryman's *Dream Songs*, and Lowell's *Notebooks*. In method and concept these works are already anticipated by such bold experiments of Whitman's as *Song of Myself* and *The Sleepers*, poems that must be counted among the great revolutionary documents of literature.

Like Whitman, Lawrence is a master of the art of incompleteness. The absence of completed form might well be regarded as a defect, and of course it has been; both Whitman and Lawrence have been frequently accused of a deficiency in art, and it has been urged that whatever else they may be—prophets, moralists, critics, celebrants—they are not artists. This has been by and large the conventional view, and what Henry James said of *Drum-Taps* in 1865—"the volume is an offense against art"—has been said, and in some quarters continues to be said, of the rest of Whitman's work, and of Lawrence's as well.[16] As poets, both were (like Wordsworth) doing something so different that criticism lacked, and perhaps still lacks, the approach or the terms to deal with it; since their most pioneering works were not "art" as critics understood the term, it was easy to conclude they were not art at all, or perhaps that they were hostile to art. It is not unusual to find critics who appear somewhat embarrassed about their liking for the poems of Whitman and Lawrence and thus speak in ways that invite detraction, as though the author wanted it clearly understood that he was not fooled—Santayana, for example, on Whitman: "This abundance of detail without organization, this wealth of perception without intelligence and of imagination without taste, makes the singularity of Whitman's genius."[17] The admirers of Whitman and Lawrence have continually been on the defensive in their efforts to establish that these poets really *are* poets, and that their work really *is* poetry, despite the apparent disregard of craftsmanship and technique. Since people have found the poems moving and significant, it seems there must be something to them that is just as good as art, or perhaps art is not what we think it is. What we often find is a willingness in critics to give up any claims for art in order to demonstrate that the poet's achievement surpassed the possibilities of conventional artistry. A. Alvarez is a case in point. He has written as well as anyone in defense of Lawrence, praising in particular the "complete truth to feeling" found in the poems. "*The whole* of Lawrence's orginality and power as a poet," he writes, "depends on the way he keeps close to his feelings. That is why he had to rid himself of conventional forms. The poems take even their shape from the feelings" (emphasis added).[18] Lawrence's poetry is praised repeatedly for its honesty and intelligence; its virtues would appear to be those of the poet, not those of art.

This suggestion would not have displeased Lawrence, who had supreme confidence in what he was doing; if others missed the point, so much the worse for them. To be praised for his "complete truth to feeling" was, after all, the main thing; for if the feeling was wrong, Lawrence insisted, nothing else could be right. Here again Lawrence takes his cue from Whitman. In an early letter (1913), writing about the rhythms of his poetry, Lawrence said this: "I think, don't you know, that my rhythms fit my mood pretty well, in the verse. And if the mood is out of joint, the rhythm often is. I have always tried to get an emotion out in its own course, without altering it. It needs the finest instinct imaginable, much finer than the skill of the craftsmen. The Japanese Yone Noguchi tried it. He doesn't quite bring it off. . . . Sometimes Whitman is perfect" (*CL*, 1. 221). Lawrence's comment comes very close to some remarks Whitman made late in his life, in 1888; like Lawrence, he was talking about the rhythms of his poetry: "Well, the lilt is all right: yes, right enough: but there's something anterior—more imperative. The first thing necessary is the thought—the rest may follow if it chooses—may play its part—must not be too much sought after. . . . Perhaps the music happens—it does no harm: I do not go in search of it" (Traubel, 1. 163).

"Perhaps the music happens"; but first things first. The thought will find its own proper poetic form, if it is true, if it is right. In certain respects Whitman and Lawrence appear to be anticipating the architectural dictum that form follows function: if the thing has the integrity of its purpose, the form will take care of itself, and it will be aesthetically beyond reproach. Design follows statement; the reverse is never true, although many poets would seem to have thought so. Lawrence was clear in his priorities. "It is the hidden *emotional* pattern that makes poetry," he wrote, "not the obvious form" (*CL*, 1. 243). Emotion has its own rhythms; it is the job of the poet to discover what they are, just as, it might be said, the sculptor discovers the shape within the stone. The poet does not so much create something as allow it to be revealed. For Whitman and for Lawrence, the deficiency of much poetry was that in its concern for conventional forms it hindered rather than advanced the process of revelation. It is enough for the poet to be present at the creation; the creative forces themselves come from without. If the poet is receptive, if he is careful not to intrude and impede, if he remains open and allows himself to be controlled, the discoveries may make themselves known. Whitman's greatest and most essential poem, it will be recalled, begins with the poet in a state of total receptivity: "I loafe and *invite* my soul, / I lean and loafe at my ease observing a spear of summer grass" (*LG*, p. 28; emphasis added). Announcing his subject, he puts aside established institutions in order to be open to the promptings of a more basic source:

> Creeds and schools in abeyance,
> Retiring back a while sufficed at what they are, but never forgotten,
> I harbor for good or bad, I *permit* to speak at every hazard,
> Nature without check with original energy.
>
> (*LG*, p. 29; emphasis added)

Lawrence's version of this opening section of "Song of Myself" is his "Song of a Man Who has Come Through":

> Not I, not I, but the wind that blows through me!
> A fine wind is blowing the new direction of Time.
> If only I let it bear me, carry me, if only it carry me!
> If only I am sensitive, subtle, oh, delicate, a winged gift!
> If only, most lovely of all, I yield myself and am borrowed
> By the fine, fine wind that takes its course through the chaos of the world
> Like a fine, an exquisite chisel, a wedge-blade inserted;
> If only I am keen and hard like the sheer tip of a wedge
> Driven by invisible blows,
> The rock will split, we shall come at the wonder, we shall find the Hesperides.
>
> Oh, for the wonder that bubbles into my soul,
> I would be a good fountain, a good well-head,
> Would blur no whisper, spoil no expression.
>
> What is the knocking?
> What is the knocking at the door in the night?
> It is somebody wants to do us harm.
>
> No, no, it is the three strange angels.
> Admit them, admit them. (*CP*, p. 250)

"Admit them": open the door. Be receptive—*invite* the soul, *permit* nature to speak, *admit* the angels. Ripeness is all, the readiness to accept what the gods may give.

## IV

The great themes of Whitman and Lawrence are closely related to their aesthetic principles. If conventional forms of verse act as barriers that prevent truth from revealing itself, the same may be said of the conventional ways of thought that compel minds into habits of perception, thus closing them to the imaginative receptivity that makes possible all true and liberating insight. In "Terra Incognita" Lawrence clearly states this essential part of his prophetic message:

> There are vast realms of consciousness still undreamed of
> vast ranges of experience, like the humming of unseen harps,
> we know nothing of, within us.
> Oh when man has escaped from the barbed-wire entanglement
> of his own ideas and his own mechanical devices
> there is a marvellous rich world of contact and sheer fluid beauty
> and fearless face-to-face awareness of now-naked life. . . .
>
> (*CP*, pp. 666–667)

In "Healing" Lawrence writes of the necessity of "freeing oneself / from the endless repetition of the mistake / which mankind at large has chosen to sanctify" (*CP*, p. 620). The mistake is the same error of perception; wrong from generation to generation, mankind distorts the nature of existence by a blind and stubborn refusal to see what is there. Misled in particular by the Platonic / Christian tradition of valuing spirit over flesh, humans debase the body when they should celebrate it; thus they despise their beings and diminish the quality of life. It is a sad mistake; for what is taken to be piety is, for Whitman and Lawrence, closer to sacrilege. "If anything is sacred," wrote Whitman, "the human body is sacred" (*LG*, p. 99); this was a theme he sounded to the end. Lawrence, equally impassioned, came to insist on the same union of physical and divine:

> God is the great urge that has not yet found a body
> but urges towards incarnation with the great creative urge.
>
> And becomes at last a clove carnation: lo! that is god!
> and becomes at last Helen, or Ninon: any lovely and generous
>   woman

at her best and most beautiful, being god, made manifest,
any clear and fearless man being god, very god.

There is no god
apart from poppies and the flying fish,
men singing songs, and women brushing their hair in the
sun. *(CP,* p. 691)

For Whitman and for Lawrence, the spirit is in the flesh. While it is possible to speak, for convenience, of a duality, there can in truth be no separation.

"The adventurer / In humanity has not conceived of a race / Completely physical in a physical world," wrote Wallace Stevens, who was trying to do precisely that. While Whitman and Lawrence could not be considered spokesmen for the *purely* physical, as they paid ample tribute to man's spiritual being, nevertheless much of their writing is a passionate effort to rehabilitate the physical and give it full due. Against the Platonic / Christian separation of matter and spirit, Whitman asserted their unity:

I will make poems of materials, for I think they are to be the
most spiritual poems,
And I will make the poems of my body and of mortality,
For I think I will then supply myself with the poems of my
soul and of immortality. *(LG,* p. 18)

Between body and soul there can be no distinction; as Whitman insisted: "I have said that the soul is not more than the body, / And I have said that the body is not more than the soul" *(LG,* p. 86). Of all Whitman's explorations, this was perhaps the most valuable for Lawrence, the discovery of the nature of our beings. In his Whitman essay he paid special tribute to this aspect of Whitman's pioneering; "Whitman", he wrote, "was the first to break the mental allegiance. He was the first to smash the old moral conception that the soul of man is something 'superior' and 'above' the flesh" *(SCAL,* p. 171). "My soul and my body are one," he proclaimed in the same essay (p. 176), thus succinctly following Whitman, who in one poem listed for more than thirty lines the various parts of the body, then concluded: "O I say that these are not the parts and poems of the body only, but of the soul, / O I say now these are the soul!" *(LG,* p. 101).

Nothing, for Whitman and Lawrence, more clearly indicated the human rejection of the body than the prevailing attitudes towards sex and death. Sex was the life-force itself; to repress sex was to distort one's being. Thus Lawrence could make such all-encompassing exhortations as the following: "Accept the sexual, physical, being of yourself, and of every other creature. Don't be afraid of it. . . . Conquer the fear of sex, and restore the natural flow" (*Phoenix II*, p. 570). "I labour always at the same things," Lawrence wrote in a letter of 1927, "to make the sex relation valid and precious, instead of shameful" (*CL*, 2. 972). Whitman could have said much the same—indeed, he often did, in one way or another: "Without shame the man I like knows and avows the deliciousness of his sex, / Without shame the woman I like knows and avows hers" (*LG*, p. 102). To Whitman as to Lawrence, sex was not just a part of life; it was at the center, the source of vitality. Late in his life (1889) Whitman commented emphatically on the matter: "Sex: sex: whether you sing or make a machine, or go to the North Pole, or love your mother, or build a house, or black shoes, or anything—anything at all—it's sex, sex, sex: sex is the root of it all: sex—the coming together of men and women: sex: sex" (Traubel, 3. 452–453). These are spirited words for a man entering his seventieth year, and they represent a deep conviction. When Whitman recalled how in 1860 Emerson had suggested deleting "certain popularly objectionable poems and passages" from *Leaves of Grass* in order to promote circulation of the book, Whitman remarked, "he did not see that if I had cut sex out I might just as well have cut everything out—the full scheme would no longer exist—it would have been violated in its most sensitive spot" (Traubel, 1. 51).

As Whitman's statements make clear, his conception of sex went beyond male / female relationships to include all human relationships, homosexual (or homoerotic) as well as heterosexual. His assertions of "the need of comrades" in the "Calamus" section of *Leaves of Grass* and elsewhere are so prominent and so familiar as to need no elaboration; Whitman is our great poet of masculine love (though not, strictly speaking, of homosexuality), and he treats the subject with frankness and a fine sense of dignity:

> Publish my name and hang up my picture as that of the tenderest lover,
> The friend the lover's portrait, of whom his friend his lover was fondest,

Who was not proud of his songs, but of the measureless ocean of love within him, and freely pour'd it forth,
Who often walk'd lonesome walks thinking of his dear friends, his lovers,
Who pensive away from one he lov'd often lay sleepless and dissatisfied at night,
Who knew too well the sick, sick dread lest the one he lov'd might secretly be indifferent to him,
Whose happiest days were far away through fields, in woods, on hills, he and another wandering hand in hand, they twain apart from other men,
Who oft as he saunter'd the streets curv'd with his arm the shoulder of his friend, while the arm of his friend rested
upon him also. (*LG*, p. 122)

Here again Lawrence followed the path that Whitman had blazed, for throughout his life he was much concerned with the erotic relationships of man to man.[19] In 1919 he wrote to Godwin Baynes: "You are a great admirer of Whitman, R. said. So am I. But I find in his '*Calamus*' and Comrades one of the clues to a real solution—the new adjustment. I believe in what he calls 'manly love,' the real implicit reliance of one man on another: as sacred a union as marriage: only it must be deeper, more ultimate than emotion and personality, cool separateness and yet the ultimate reliance."[20] Here and there in his letters Lawrence touches upon the theme; as early as 1913 he writes: "I should like to know why nearly every man that approaches greatness tends to homosexuality, whether he admits it or not: so that he loves the *body* of a man better than the body of a woman" (*CL*, l. 251). In his fiction the most notable exploration of homoeroticism is probably *Women in Love*, and while writing this novel Lawrence himself may have been pursuing an active homosexual relationship, though the pursuit appears to have been unsuccessful.[21]

Whitman, of course, was much more open and receptive, much more willing to give of himself, in his relationships than Lawrence, who seemed always to be trying to determine how he could form deep attachments and at the same time retain his fierce independence—a contradictory and impossible task, as it turned out. When others made demands on Lawrence or expected some sort of emotional response from him, he recoiled, frequently in disgust and detestation. Lawrence was not designed for intimacy. Nevertheless, the ideal of full and perfect human relationships remained, at least for a time; it was only later in his life that he gave up his Whitmanesque quest for "love of comrades," in particular for the "eternal union with a man" that Birkin speaks of at the end of *Women in Love*. Even when he was attacking Whitman in the third and final version of his *Studies in Classic American Literature* essay, published in 1923, he could still refer to "Comradeship" as "extreme and alone, touching the confines of death. Something terrible to bear, terrible to be responsible for. Even Walt Whitman felt it. The soul's last and most poignant responsibility, the responsibility of comradeship, of manly love" (*SCAL*, p. 169).

The fullest expression of Lawrence's homoeroticism comes in the novels; in the poems he holds back, perhaps because this theme is too intimate and too revealing for even so intimate and revealing a poet as Lawrence. Despite his verbal outpouring, Lawrence could be extremely reticent where personal relationships were concerned, and he was capable of determined self-restraint. Even Whitman, who explored the theme of homoeroticism with unparalleled boldness, stopped short of such complete revelation as may be found, for example, in the poetry of Allen Ginsberg or Paul Goodman. Whitman's method was generally to hint at a revelation ("I am not what you supposed, but far different," *LG*, p. 115), then pull away and make his exit ("Even while you should think you had unquestionably caught me, behold! / Already you see I have escaped from you," *LG*, p. 116). Of all the things that Whitman might have said in the closing lines of his greatest poem, what he *does* say, as though it were of conclusive importance, is that he remains as elusive as ever:

> Failing to fetch me at first keep encouraged,
> Missing me one place search another,
> I stop somewhere waiting for you. (*LG*, p. 89)

The reader is left in solitude; and while the poet says he is waiting, it seems more likely that he is hiding.

In addition to his elusiveness, Whitman took further care to obscure the record with assertions of heterosexuality by claiming to have fathered six illegitimate children, none of whom seems ever to have existed. Still, the extraordinary thing is that his poetry celebrates such a *complete* range of human relationships, including the homoerotic. There Whitman was a pioneer, and Lawrence a dedicated follower.

## V

As much as anyone's, Whitman's poetry is concerned with the possibilities of body and spirit. Sex is central, in all its wide and varied manifestations, and so is death, that finality shared by all. Although Whitman is widely (and rightly) regarded as one of our supreme writers on death—"a very great poet, of the end of life" Lawrence called him (*SCAL*, p. 170)—the subject appears in his works much less frequently than one would suppose; his reputation comes largely from the importance of death as a theme in the great poems that people know if they know any Whitman at all: "Song of Myself," "When Lilacs Last in the Dooryard Bloom'd and "Out of the Cradle Endlessly Rocking." Even if Whitman had never mentioned the subject elsewhere, in these poems it is treated with such conviction and such mastery that he would be regarded as he is, "a very great poet, of the end of life."

Lawrence's words apply to himself as well as to Whitman, for in his final years he too became a great poet of the end of life, in no small measure because of the strong presence of Whitman. In the *Last Poems* (published posthumously in 1932), Whitman's influence, so long essential in forming Lawrence's mind, and so instrumental in determining certain aspects of his versification, comes to enter into the poems at their most basic levels of rhythm and tone. Whitman's example had, of course, pointed Lawrence toward free verse, and in *Birds, Beasts and Flowers*, published in 1923, the Whitman influence was clearly visible in mannerisms of style; but in the *Last Poems* it becomes not so much an influence as a generating force. The assimilation is complete. Throughout this book, and most notably in the great death poems, "Bavarian Gentians" and "The Ship of Death" (and perhaps in the lesser-known, but very fine, "Shadows"), Lawrence's verse achieves a new, truly Whitmanesque (yet individual) sonority; it becomes measured, stately, celebratory, and at the same time passionate and personal, deeply felt and deeply moving. The quick nervous rhythms of *Look! We Have Come Through!* and the earlier blank verse poems have been replaced by tones of calm assurance as Lawrence, like Whitman, looks at death directly and accepts it as no more (and no less) than a stage of existence, a necessary passing through that gives meaning to our days:

> Sing the song of death, O sing it!
> for without the song of death, the song of life
> becomes pointless and silly.    (*CP*, p. 723)

"Death's not sad, when one has lived," Lawrence wrote in a 1925 letter (*CL*, 2. 851), returning as he does so often to his sense of *life*—of vitality, "quickness"—for reassurance and justification. The meditations on death in the *Last Poems* represent a final triumph of Whitman's example and Lawrence's creative force. These poems could not have been written without Whitman; but they are distinctly Lawrence's poems.

Nowhere in Whitman is there such a sustained meditation on death as in Lawrence's, "The Ship of Death," a poem in which Lawrence passes through various moods and perspectives as he follows the subject through its changes. As he concludes, however, he comes to see death from a perspective that owes much to Whitman. For a moment he seems to have reached the end: "And everything is gone, the body is gone / completely under, gone, entirely gone" (*CP*, p. 719). Unexpectedly there arises a new beginning:

> Wait, wait, the little ship
> drifting, beneath the deathly ashy grey
> of a flood-dawn.
>
> Wait, wait! even so, a flush of yellow
> and strangely, O chilled wan soul, a flush of rose.
>
> A flush of rose, and the whole thing starts again.
>                         (*CP*, p. 720)

What is starting, however, is not an afterlife, but the "cruel dawn of coming back to life out of oblivion" (*CP*, p. 720). In his last years Lawrence may have imagined himself on the point of death many times and perhaps experienced something like the new beginning he describes. Though Lawrence loved life, the return to existence as he portrays it in "The Ship of Death" is greeted not with jubilation, but with something of a resigned shrug: "the whole thing starts again." Whitman would not have put it this way, though the attitude toward death (rather than life) derives in large measure from his own celebrations; for this return falls short of the eternal renewal promised by oblivion: in death the individual returns to the essential, inexhaustible quickness, the great sea in which all things are born, all things die. In Whitman's words, "All goes onward and outward, nothing collapses, / And to die is different from what any one supposed, and luckier" (*LG*, p. 35). For Lawrence and Whitman both, death is to be accepted, even to be celebrated, because it is part of the movement of life; the fact of death demonstrates the vitality that impels the universe: "The smallest sprout shows there is really no death, / And if there ever was it led forward life, and does not wait at the end to arrest it" (*LG*, p. 34).

It is fitting that at the very end of his life, in the last months, when he was writing his final book, at a time when his suffering and anxiety might have caused him to turn to bitterness and cynicism, Lawrence turned instead to Whitmanesque affirmation and joy. The central passage is well known, and justly so; it is the conclusion of *Apocalypse*, and it deserves to be quoted in full:

> For man, the vast marvel is to be alive. For man, as for flower and beast and bird, the supreme triumph is to be most vividly, most perfectly alive. Whatever the unborn and the dead may know, they cannot know the beauty, the marvel of being alive in the flesh. The dead may look after the afterwards. But the magnificent here and now of life in the flesh is ours, and ours alone, and ours only for a time. We ought to dance with rapture that we should be alive and in the flesh, and part of the living, incarnate cosmos. That I am part of the earth my feet know perfectly, and my blood is part of the sea. My soul knows that I am part of the human race, my soul is an organic part of the great human soul, as my spirit is part of my nation. In my very own self, I am part of my family. There is nothing of me that is alone and absolute except my mind, and we shall find that the mind has no existence by itself, it is only the glitter of the sun on the surface of the waters.
>
> So that my individualism is really an illusion. I am a part of the great whole, and I can never escape. But I *can* deny my connections, break them, and become a fragment. Then I am wretched.
>
> What we want is to destroy our false, inorganic connections, especially those related to money, and re-establish the living organic connections, with the cosmos, the sun and earth, with mankind and nation and family. Start with the sun, and the rest will slowly, slowly happen.[22]

Whitman's great themes are here, and Lawrence makes them his own. Whatever he has said about the mysterious beauty of death—and nothing is denied—Lawrence comes back to the center, to the quickness of life, the vitality of the moment. To be *alive*: that is enough, and more than enough; the gift of being requires nothing more than itself. The thought, of course, is Whitman's:

> I exist as I am, that is enough,
> If no other in the world be aware I sit content,
> And if each and all be aware I sit content.
>
> (*LG*, p. 48)

At the close of *Apocalypse*, at the close of his life, Lawrence gathers strength in the reassurance of Whitman's great prophetic message. In one last magnificent outpouring he sounds the essential themes: the mysterious beauty of life in a physical world; the joy of living, the mere being; the inescapable bonds of the human community; the merging of the one in the many; the organic relationships connecting all that exists, the smallest part with the greatest, each part with every other part. As *Apocalypse* shows, the presence that guided Lawrence throughout his life was with him to give direction at the end.

CHAPTER SEVEN

# Lawrence and the Nietzschean Matrix

## KINGSLEY WIDMER

Much of D. H. Lawrence can only be understood within the context of a most perplexing and exasperating tradition of sensibility, nihilistic and counter-nihilistic prophecy *in extremis*. Yet in a parochialism often almost as evident in American literary study as in British, the continuities with Lawrence frequently come out as some sort of English-y "great tradition."[1] His significant forerunners, therefore, are the major nineteenth-century British novelists, from George Eliot to Thomas Hardy.[2] A somewhat less narrowly moralistic view of the inheritance allows for the Brontës and the English Romantics; a rather more suspicious perspective perceives some sources in more eccentric writer-prophets, whether Carlyle or the Midlands homosexual apologist Edward Carpenter.[3] A less intellectual provincialism submerges Lawrence in his lower-class Midlands background—"the coal-miner's son"—whether somewhat patronizingly, as with his early supporters, or somewhat sentimentally, as with his more recent biographers.[4] The partial truth of these emphases helps to confirm their inadequate perspectives. Lawrence's fictions, slowly evolving out of conventional origins, obviously did relate to those of his British predecessors. He also certainly had some continuities with the Romantics, especially Blake (and Whitman), though he was usually rather dismissive of them.[5] Surely he was marked by his provincial origins and his lower-class resentments in a class-ridden society, and especially marred by his mother's petty bourgeois repressions and aspirations, beyond his role as a rather priggish schoolteacher. But too much emphasis on these sources and lineaments must miss much of Lawrence's peculiarity. And thus one insufficiently recognizes this raging man's rebellions against his origins and, more generally, against English society and culture. Parochially oriented criticism encourages misestimations of Lawrence's cultural role. Lawrence will be better understood and responded to when seen as a *revolté*, an outsider prophet, belonging to a different and darker matrix of sensibility.[6]

## I  *Lawrence's Education in Nietzsche*

Now it is often granted that some other intellectual "influences" reached Lawrence in his later twenties (his intellectual and artistic maturation was relatively slow), including from 1912 on his German-reared wife's enthusiasms for Nietzsche and Freud. But clear evidence, repeatedly noted long ago, points out that the influence of Nietzsche on Lawrence was pre-Frieda von Richthofen Weekley.[7] Lawrence's crucial editor-mentor, Ford Madox Ford, described Lawrence amid his Eastwood friends about 1910: "All the while the young people were talking about Nietzsche and Wagner and Leopardi and Flaubert and Karl Marx and Darwin."[8] Ford's accounts, it is generally acknowledged, are often fanciful or hyperbolic, and so the details here may not be literal, though there seems little reason to suspect the general direction of his report about the intellectual breadth and energy of these Lawrencean provincials. But note, too, in context the confirming tone of surprise in Ford. Like many successful and fashionable *literati*, he did not expect such intellectual vitality in the outlands and out-classes (though one could well have, given the effects of the earlier Education Acts, access to libraries and inexpensive books for seekers out of a puritan background, and early twentieth-century social and cultural ferment). The smug insularity, now as well as then, of established intellectual circles (even with a relatively open and sympathetic figure such as Ford) may be part of the issue when we talk about "traditions."

Otherwise put, a significant part of Lawrence's intellectual development took place "amid the neo-Nietzschean clatter" (Pound, *Mauberley*) of the years when "the last metaphysician" was having considerable literary effect in England (on G. B. Shaw, W. B. Yeats, Wyndham Lewis, J. C. Powys and others). More than a generation ago, comparativists pointed to the passage in the memoirs of Jessie Chambers, Lawrence's adolescent girl friend, about his early school teaching days: "It was in the library at

Croydon that Lawrence found Nietzsche. He never mentioned him directly to me, nor suggested that I should read him, but I began to hear about the 'Will to Power,' and perceived that he had come upon something new and engrossing."[9] While the account is missing something (Chambers, if Lawrence had not mentioned Nietzsche, must have had other evidence—seeing the books? comments from others?), her point is confirmed elsewhere. In a stilted and mawkish early autobiographical story about his first love (Jessie, the Miriam of *Sons and Lovers*, here called Muriel), "A Modern Lover" (completed by 1911, but probably earlier in genesis), Lawrence has his "superior" and priggish young protagonist summarize his intellectual education as having *started* with Brontë and Eliot, then moving through Russian and French writers, with Nietzsche as a concluding high point.[10] Some Nietzschean elements may be recognized several years later in Lawrence's very bad second novel, *The Trespasser* (published 1912), not only in its references to Nietzsche (and Heine, Turgenev, Wagner, Nihilism, etc.), and in its motifs of battle of wills, art-as-intensity, and the inadequacy of middle-class emotions, but also in the murkiness around the suicide of its guilty-adulterous music teacher, Siegmund, a later German-romantic protagonist.[11]

In a more mature book review (1913), Lawrence praises Nietzsche for "demolishing" the "Christian religion as it stood."[12] In his "Study of Thomas Hardy" (written in 1914 but not published in his lifetime), he wrote of one major style of lover, of what we now call the *macho* male, in his "passion": "the female administers to him. He feels full of blood, he walks the earth like a Lord. And it is to this state that Nietzsche aspires in *Wille zur Macht*." But perhaps defensively, and in spite of obvious similarities to his own views, and to his recurrent fictional "demon lovers," he attacks this Nietzscheanism as really a *fear* of the female which results in the compensatory *roué* compulsiveness. Thus, concludes Lawrence, "the *Wille zur macht* is a spurious feeling."[13] Somewhat more positive is Lawrence's use of Nietzschean terms and arguments in showing the male inadequacy of Egbert in the story "England, My England" (1915).[14] But whether arguing against, or counter-arguing with, Nietzsche, Lawrence continues to project his somewhat canted view of he who "philosophized with a hammer."

In Lawrence's novels of the Great War period, the Nietzscheanism is also more than a little evident. In *The Rainbow* (written 1912–15) the last third of the ragged family saga centers on Ursula

Brangwen, Lawrence's version (beyond the slighter Clara in *Sons and Lovers*) of the "modern woman" struggling for defiant self-definition. Rather improbably for a provincial adolescent and then elementary school teacher, she becomes the vehicle for some Nietzschean declarations. While still a child, Lawrence gives her an emphatic rejection of Christian *caritas* and the humble moral imperative. "And she *didn't* want to do what the gospels said. She didn't want to be poor."[15] Furthermore, "Nor could one turn the other cheek." When her sister slaps her, she tries it, gets slapped again, and "went meekly away." But she soon revolts in anger and shame and beats her sister, feeling "unchristian but clean." In a summation which would be quite in place in *The Genealogy of Morals*, "There was something unclean and degrading about this humble side of Christianity."[16]

Like a good adolescent Nietzschean, Ursula then has fantasies of being an aristocratic lady. However, I am not suggesting that all of her defiance of conventional Christianity—as in her later blasphemously insisting on sexual foreplay in a cathedral—need be related to the anti-Christian philosopher with whom Lawrence had for some time been fascinated. Lawrence, of course, had good personal reasons from his own background and society as well as other intellectual influences for rejecting the usual religious prohibitions and impositions. But certainly the unexpected, and hardly prepared for, political statements that Ursula is given near the end of the novel are of Nietzschean cast. In the process of rejecting her lover, the conventional colonial army officer Anton Skrebensky, she announces: "I shall be glad to leave England. Everything is so meagre and paltry, it is so unspiritual—I hate democracy." Defending herself against Anton's hostile response, she goes on: "Only the greedy and ugly people come to the top in a democracy . . . because they're the only people who will push themselves there. Only degenerate races are democratic."[17] Instead she wants an "aristocracy" of the spiritually superior—or, implicitly, in her psychological castration of Anton, some more obscurely fulfilling potency, some transcending *Übermensch*.

But such fantasy longings don't quite get fulfilled in *Women in Love* (1920, but mostly written 1915–17), though the partly reconceived Ursula does marry a dubiously superior man and flees degenerate England. She no longer incongruously spouts such doctrines; they have shifted to her new lover, an obvious Lawrence *persona* (though vaguely upper class in education, private income, and social-erotic life), Rupert Birkin. Typically, again some of his Nietzscheanism is put in reverse ways, as in the cancelled opening section of the novel, since published as "Foreword to *Women in Love*," where the homosexuality of the book's protagonist was made more explicit. Here we find Birkin "holding forth against Nietzsche."[18] The crux of his attack, central doctrine to all the later Lawrence, rests on the polarity between "desire" and "will": "A man cannot create desire in himself, nor cease at will from desiring. Desire, in any shape or form, is primal, whereas the will is secondary, derived. The will can destroy, but it cannot create."[19]

But in the rest of the novel Lawrence partly creates a straw-Nietzsche. For example, Ursula describes Gerald Crich spurring his horse until it bled at a railroad crossing as "a lust for bullying—a real *Wille zur Macht*—so base, so petty."[20] Birkin ostensibly accepts the anti-Nietzschean point: "I agree that the *Wille zur Macht* is a base and petty thing," yet he goes on to argue for a willful male dominance quite like it, though redefined in French to slip ambiguously under Nordic bullying—"a *volonté de pouvoir*, if you like, a will to ability." By such verbal slight of hand he confirms the essential Nietzscheanism.

"Will" is an obsessive subject in *Women in Love*, as in many of Lawrence's fictions, and one which requires a sense that Lawrence is both drawing upon and qualifying the philosophy of Will to Power. Apparently we are to understand Gerald Crich, in the chapter "The Industrial Magnate," as the bad-Nietzschean, for "what he wanted was the pure fulfillment of his own will."[21] In Lawrence's condemnation of the industrial system, Gerald moves toward this by substituting impersonal management and dehumanized relationships—what Max Weber called "modern rationalization"—for the old paternalistic order in the family mines. Something like this is often noted, but what is not linked to it is Lawrence's equally vehement rejection of the old order in his Nietzschean attack on the Christian ethic of the previous generation's paternalism. For what that encouraged was "the whining, parasitic foul human beings who came crawling after charity, and feeding on the living body of the public like lice."[22] Lawrence, then, hates the "will to power" of the new industrial order but also hates the Christian antithesis which Nietzsche so thoroughly excoriated. The double-condemnation, of both traditional and rationalized power, in this prophetic matrix can only point to a utopian vision of a quite different order. And so, elsewhere, Lawrence does.

In the concluding pattern of *Women in Love* Gerald's will-to-live breaks—a somewhat obscure fictional argument, I think, suggesting that his will has been defeated by a false passion, by the even more destructive willfullness of modern art (Gudrun and Loerke), and by some lack of organic vitality. Yet Lawrence is less attacking than partly redefining the will to mastery. When Birkin demands that Ursula give up *her* "assertive *will*" and surrender to him,[23] she rightly sees this as a demand of bullying and domineering male will, though she gives in out of need and love. Lawrence has hardly succeeded in transforming the Will to Power into a clearly different "superiority," vitality, "fuller being," or "dark power," however much he attacks will as cerebral, manipulative, destructive. He simply struggles with variations within the Nietzschean matrix. Or, as we can note yet another version of the argument from another novel of the same period (and centering on yet another slavish submission of a woman to male will)—*The Lost Girl*: "The puerile world went on crying out for a new Jesus. . . .When what was wanted was a Dark Master from the underworld."[24]

The icy will of annihilation that killed Gerald Crich (among others) must somehow be countered by a will-annihilating dark passionate . . . will. "Will" for Lawrence is a frequent and mostly negative term, however, used in describing his recurrent witch figures of "willful" women (obviously based in the domineering maternal), and to characterize cerebral conscience over-riding the fuller passional (for an extreme example: the suicidal Ethel using "will" against her sexuality in "None of That,"[25] as well as the murderous Hermione in *Women in Love*). And Lawrence frequently uses "will," from Gerald Crich on, to characterize modern industrial civilization, which inherently produced the Great War and other destructiveness instead of more organic community. True, a few times Lawrence attempts to salvage "will" from destructiveness, as in his distinction in a later essay: "We have a confused idea that *will* and power are somehow identical. We think we can have a will to power."[26] But since he finds authentic power in the passional, as in unwilled sexual desire and intense individuality, he condemns Will to Power again as just "bullying." Apparently Lawrence felt he was attacking Nietzsche who may sometimes have used Will to Power in this way but, it is often and reasonably argued, was more significantly using it in a way rather closer to Lawrence's view of power as richer individual *being*.²⁷ The pattern, then, of Lawrence's overt relation to Nietzsche might be summarized thus: discovery and influence in a crucial period of his intellectual development as he was breaking away from his provincial origins, then reinforcement several years later by his wife's ideological enthusiasm, developing into an obsessive dialectic both as a domestic counter-assertion and as a variant propounding of his own very similar ontology. In essential ways, Lawrence had thus become an English Nietzsche.

## II  *The Prophet of Dionysus*

Some of this appears quite clearly in a relatively late story placed in the post-Great War German scene, "The Border Line" (1924).²⁸ On the more personal level of motivation, the story savages Lawrence's longtime friend, the critic Middleton Murry (here named Phillip) for his erotic involvement with Frieda Lawrence (here named Katherine); in the fictional version, she has married him after the Great War death of her first husband (here named Alan—a British army officer who oddly serves a recurrent fantasy projection of Lawrence's²⁹). Alan–Lawrence is an amoralist Nietzschean *Übermensch*, a "born lord" who "had an weird innate conviction that he was beyond ordinary judgment," a "real man" with a special sense of "fate." Alan had gone to war with a cool superiority since "only the cold strength of a man, accepting the destiny of destruction, could see the human flow through the chaos and beyond to a new outlet. But the chaos first, and the long rage of destruction." Passional lover as well as Nietzschean nihilist, he had the very *macho* eroticism I earlier quoted Lawrence as condemning in Nietzsche; he showed "an implacable pride and strength" and "expected a woman to bow down to him." Yet he also had explicitly a "contempt of Nietzsche," apparently because his wife "adored" the similar thinker. The wife, after a vision of anti-Christian apocalypse, has a sexual consummation in the woods with the demon-ghost of her dead husband, and, again in the marital hotel bed as her craven intellectual husband fearfully dies. This second-rate ghost tale of sexual revenge clearly affirms the Nietzscheanism it ostensibly denies.

Lawrence, partly following Nietzsche (and also earlier romantic lineages), exalts the dark ecstatically erotic pagan deity, Dionysus, who in Christian iconography merged with other devils to produce the demon-lover, as with Alan in "The Border Line."[30] It is a recurrent figure in Lawrence's fictions. But his propounding of the Dionysian also took other forms, as we might briefly note in his notorious "leadership novels." *Aaron's Rod* (first published in 1922, though partly written in 1917) never directly mentions Nietzsche but provides an overlay for some of his views.[31] Written with sloppy haste, it is a half-hearted, ideological picaresque novel about an ex-coal miner become flautist who wanders, questing and despairing, in London and then in postwar Italy after deserting his family. His quasi-homoerotic companion and intellectual guru, Rawdon Lilly, an obvious Lawrence *persona*, is a badly unrealized figure, who egomaniacally asserts "a certain belief in himself as a saviour" because he is a superior man of true "knowledge" whose "soul was against the whole world" as it was.[32] His sermonizing includes some racist ranting, raging condemnations of modern mass society, and near mystical demands for "sacred" individualism to replace the dead absolute, now "there's no God outside." With inadequate dramatization, we also learn that "Love was a battle in which each party strove for the mastery of the other's soul," no doubt reflecting Lawrence's domestic difficulties with Frieda (just as Zarathustra's pronouncements on women in the later sections of that work seem to reflect Nietzsche's rejection by Lou Salomé). This is to be resolved by putting down willful women and redirecting the female: "The woman must now submit," though in a way that goes beyond "slavery" to a "deep unfathomable free submission."[33]

But it is not altogether unfathomable since the subordination of eros to power serves a larger subordination of "love" which also includes *caritas*. Early and late in the book Lawrence not only inverts values but attacks, Nietzsche-style, their traditional Western base. As Aaron says, "To hell with good-will. It was more hateful than ill-will." Or, as a more elaborate Lilly–Lawrence lecture has it:

> The ideal of love, the ideal that it is better to give than to receive, the ideal of liberty, the ideal of the brotherhood of man, the ideal of the sanctity of human life, the ideal of what we call goodness, charity, benevolence ... all the whole bee-hive of ideals—has got the modern bee-disease, and gone putrid, stinking.[34]

Precisely as with Nietzsche, this rejected Christian-engendered morality is seen as having "its logical sequence in Socialism and equality." But we might also see the Nietzschean–Lawrencean view, as a thoughtful Jewish character in the fiction notes, as "nihilism." Lilly–Lawrence also insists, like Dostoyevsky's Grand Inquisitor, that in consequence the masses "will elect for themselves a proper and healthy and energetic slavery," "I mean a real committal of the life-issue of inferior beings to the responsibility of a superior being."[35] Yet within a page of this, Lawrence's spokesman anarchistically undercuts the argument by asserting the absolute of holy individualism and denouncing the "*bullying*" again of the individual as the ultimate hateful vice, though it would seem absolutely necessary for "healthy" submission (even for Hegel's "happy slave").

*Aaron's Rod* concludes with more of Lawrence's Nietzschean attack on "hard morality": "Religion and love—and all that. It's a disease now." The inevitable "recoil" from the love-disease becomes violent and horrific, supposedly including the symbolically castrating bombing earlier in the narrative—the social love-ethic itself the source of modern terrorism. So, goes Lawrence's argument, man must leave off the "love-whooshing" and "passionately" embrace the deep, dark "power motive."[36] That is, men, as well as the more obvious needing women, must "submit to some greater soul than theirs," submerge themselves in the "heroic soul," voluntarily, magically, in order to re-establish values against the nihilism of "love" and achieve wholeness and purpose.

From a libertarian perspective, I hold, this is no "transvaluation" of values but, rather, a re-mystification of the disease of love-control in the form of hero-control. Probably Lawrence's Nietzschean hero-worship and will-to-power can partly be related to personal problems he gave to Aaron: alienation, sexual ambivalence, deracination and despairing illness. More generally, of course, Lawrence's extreme ideology reflects in an ugly way the Great War "disillusion as never before" (Pound) and other horrors of hopelessness in Western mass society against which it makes desperate assertions. Post-war flight from England, then from Europe, was to provide Lawrence little relief, as his further Nietzschean ideologizing in his authority-longing next novel, *Kangaroo*, was to show.[37]

*Kangaroo* (written hastily in a few weeks in 1922)[38] also suffers from shapelessness and ranting, along with some not especially knowledgeable Australian tourist stuff, some intense descriptive passages and digressive memories.[39] The latter include Lawrence's account of his extreme revulsion even to being examined for conscription, from which he was eliminated for poor health—pathetic prelude to his postwar fantasies of projection into military officers (in contrast, Nietzsche, until he was invalided out, rather strongly identified with his military submission). The Australian novel also has fragmented bits of the Lawrences' marital struggle of wills and Lawrence's skittishness about whether he was a cultivated English "gentleman" or still of his "working class" origins (an issue he was not to make serious efforts to resolve until the declassed outsider Mellors of the third version of *Lady Chatterley's Lover*).[40] And it is riddled with a half-repressed homosexuality as Lawrence both yearns for and revolts against matiness and mergence with male heroes. In short, the novel chatters all too much about Lawrence's egotism and ambivalent sexuality and other illnesses.

The synthetic political issue for the touring English essayist Lawrence *persona*, Somers, concerns ostensible socialists and a fascistic nationalist group, "the diggers," led by a rich homosexual Jewish lawyer nicknamed Kangaroo, who dies from a combination of political terrorism and Lawrence–Somers' ambivalent rejection. While much of the politics comes out as ill-conceived bluster, it does display Lawrence's demands for a passional-religious "new bond between men" to transvalue the loss of human communion and community, an enlargement of the mystic blood-brotherhood of *Women in Love*, but Lawrence's spokesman skittishly turns away from the homoerotic politics. Similarly, he longs for apocalyptic change in the empty modern world but then disdainfully notes, "I'm afraid . . . that, like Nietzsche, I no longer believe in great events." And he is full of spiteful demands for authoritarianism, though he finds both its "socialist" and "fascist" forms false because based yet again on the dead ethic of the "will-to-love."[41]

Fused with this is the attack on "mob" morality, in which Lawrence outdoes Nietzsche on "herd morality," defined as that "collection of all the weak souls . . . that lusts to glut itself with blind destructive power." But it is truly a "dark God" speaking through Somers–Lawrence, as with the description of the English people: "They are *canaille*, carrion-eating, filthy mouthed *canaille*, like deadmen-devouring jackals. I wish to God I could kill them. I wish I had the power to blight them . . . slay them in thousands and thousands," and on and on.[42] Hatred here does not produce the art it sometimes does in Lawrence. In utter rage against the "compulsions" of the Great War, he incoherently insists on greater compulsions. Since those of the war, and industrial-bourgeois societies more generally, were costumed in benevolence, we have again, as in *Aaron's Rod*, the central Nietzschean rejection of nihilistic idealism: "For the idea, or ideal of Love, Self-Sacrifice, Humanity united in love, in brotherhood, in peace—all this is dead."[43] This includes, of course, the Christianity out of which it developed and, in the rather ragged development of *Kangaroo*, the socialism and fascism seen as still deploying the same mass-love idealism. The argument, I suggest, is implicitly powerful: many of the massive crimes of Western civilization have come in the guise of benevolent idealism—especially those Lawrence was so sensitive to, such as the destruction of the natural order, the exploitative mass industrial-urban ugliness, the pathological great wars, and the sensual warping and pervasive passional inauthenticity. But it cannot be said that this, or related, fiction develops the issues with much subtlety or other persuasiveness.

In his rage to demystify destructive western civilization Lawrence is ready to re-mystify "the great life-urge which we call God."[44] By an old logic of mystagoguery, that cosmic vitalism is displaced into supposedly superior men, though this fiction's examples, be they the left and right demagogues or the Napoleon and Caesar of the rhetoric, grossly undercut the argument. And in the texture of *Kangaroo* (as in much of Nietzsche's more poetic writings) the exaltation of the hero all too obviously displays its source in the psychological and social defensiveness of the weak outcast, the author. Somers–Lawrence rhetorically insists on the "aristocratic principle, the *innate* difference between people," because little actual difference is evident.[45] Lawrence, that is, displays the very symptoms of that major illness of social-political morality which Nietzsche acutely perceived as *ressentiment*.[46] Perhaps fortunately, Lawrence partly undercuts his symptomatic bombast not only by its over-statement but by pyrrhic dramatization—his redeeming skepticism, so evident in the endings of most of his novels. The intelligence of part of Lawrence's sensibility goes beyond his most fervent ideologies, which is often what makes him fascinating.

In yet another side of him, his rather desperately over-weening individualism—"the self is absolute"—Lawrence restates, more accurately this time, the positive meaning of the Nietzschean Will to Power: "It is a will-to-live in the further sense, a will-to-change, a will-to-evolve, a will towards the further creation of the self."[47] Furthermore, by some creative "polarity" of agonistic conflict between the spiritual aristocrats who assert this Will to Power and the unwilling "mass," a new stage in civilized "evolution" will be reached, and hence a new "*being*." This is the most positive, and possibly persuasive, version of the Will to Power. But the ontology remains an abstract speculation, in personal identification as well as narrative fact. (Somers flees Australia for America, as did Lawrence), the vitalist author rejects most actual possibilities, and certainly all social-political movements, to hold on only to "one's own isolate being." That inevitably returns one to a defiant nihilism, that is, the explicit denial of the adequacy of "any meaning," which really should be at the heart of what we mean by the Nietzschean matrix.[48] The flight from Western idealistic nihilism comes full circle in the defiant and despairing outcast last individual.

Lawrence tried again and again to bring this individual into a communion and community, to resolve the defeating isolation by translating the Will to Power into social-political mythology. But while it may be a credit to heroic effort, it certainly results in repeated fictional failure. In his next, and in many ways most repulsive novel, *The Plumed Serpent* (completed 1925), a work written in physical and moral illness, the very entitling image draws not just on the Aztec mythology of Quetzalcoatl but on Nietzsche's recurrent image of snake and bird in *Thus Spake Zarathustra*. In both sources, the trope suggests a fusion of polarities of earth and sky, higher and lower impetuses, though it should also be acknowledged that Lawrence's awareness of the need for community gave a different direction from Nietzsche's near solipsistic metapsychology.[49]

But the transvaluatory fusions in *The Plumed Serpent* mostly come out as high bombast for low impetuses. The desperate individualist is this time weakened into a fortyish Anglo-Irish widow, Kate Leslie, in Mexico, yearning, in Lawrence's somewhat patronizing perspective, to join a regenerative movement. One crux is a confused conversion experience: "Ye must be born again. Out of the fight with the octopus of life, the dragon of degenerate or incomplete existence, one must win this soft bloom of being." She hungers "to be merged in desire beyond desire, to be gone in the body beyond the individualism," a "morning star" female goddess in submission to the dark sun of generic man.[50] More literally, she self-hatingly subordinates herself to two fanatical thugs, Ramón and Cipriano, murderers who peddle a made-up Aztec Methodism and its authoritarian politico-religiosity.[51] This largely consists of a ritualism developed at intolerable length and with a vulgar literalism in very bad prose–poetry—the main traditions here being neither anthropological nor philosophical but Lawrence's early protestantism and other sub-literary languages and longings. Kate submerges intelligence, sensibility, sexual gratification (the by now notorious "Aphrodite of the foam" attack on "clitoral" orgasm) and despairing selfhood.[52] While there are intermittent bits of Lawrence's perceptiveness and descriptive power (usually at the start of chapters before the hysterical ritualization overcomes all), the novel is mostly ugly and bad, most importantly because caught up in the "fathomless lust of resentment, a demonish hatred of life itself," which it only pretends to transform into a new communion.[53]

Even considered as a Nietzschean "thought experiment" or a Lawrencean "shedding" of sickness, *The Plumed Serpent* defeats the intelligence and sensitivity of the anguished revaluation of values which, after all, provides the justification of such efforts. Iconoclasm, the matrix's real strength, reverses into icon–masturbation and pseudo-myths of megalomaniac resentment. That, indeed, is the darkness of prophecy.

As the darkness of madness approached, Nietzsche ecstatically identified himself as *both* sides of his dialectic of icons, as both pagan and Christian, as both rapturous idealist and hero overcome, as "the Crucified One" and "Dionysus." Approaching the darkness of death with his last novella, *The Escaped Cock* (1928, retitled *The Man Who Died*), Lawrence combined basically the same tropes and commitments into a blasphemously fornicating Christ who rejects his messianic social-moral role for a life-affirming myth of endless rebellion.[54] The disruptive demon of fertility and passion no longer pretends to be a leader, but a permanently and properly disestablished Dionysus.

III  *Lawrence as the English Nietzsche*

Surely some of the conjunction between Lawrence and Nietzsche appears larger, that is, more personal and basic, than the "influences" and the related practices of Will to Power and Dionysian ideologizing that I have partly summarized. They had strikingly similar sensibilities. Both writers came out of puritanic-pietistic Christian backgrounds enforced by domineering mothers.[55] Both rebelled against family, God and ethos, yet remained significantly understandable in terms of radical protestant individualism, including its extremes of moral righteousness, howevever inverted, driving them to reactive revelations. They dramatically polemicized against Christianity—Zarathustra's "God is dead" and Lawrence's "the Almighty has vacated, abdicated, climbed down"[56]—and made blasphemous revelations of the "idealistic" sensual perversions, moral nihilisms and metaphysical pathos in fungoid growth from the Christian heritage. Yet each insistently lusted after new-old gods and revived pagan demons. This psychological-moral-transcendental struggle took on sometimes heroic (and sometimes grotesque) proportions in which both over-reached into megalomania—sometimes literally confusing themselves with God-Christ and Pan-Dionysus—as they desperately sought to be the angry last prophets of decadent and destructive Western civilization.

Heroic, surely, and this is partly why we continue to make much of these often messy and confusing writers. But we also should not forget some of the grotesque context. Both heroic figures were from childhood on frail, sickly, often grievously ill. For the larger part of their productive years these invalided ex-schoolteachers were compulsive wanderers in parallel "oscillations between north and south"[57]—this itself provided a moral dialectic for both—in an ostensible search for health which was really an insistent self-exile unto madness and death. Though weak, both lusted after heroic manliness. This hero-worship must be seen as a mixture of the personally compensatory, the ambiguously homoerotic with an idealistic Philia, and a hatred of the smugly dominant bourgeois mediocrity which they attempted to subvert with a made-up aesthetic-aristocratic utopianism. The shrill demands for the "aristocratic principle" and the "vital hero" (Lawrence), for the "*Übermensch*" and "nobility" (Nietzsche), and other metaphors of the ambiguous philosophy of the "Will to Power" (both), in demonic reversal of the God of Love and his denatured ethic, often lead to the horrendously contradictory. These darkened prophets iconoclastically deny all existent authority, often with a devastating insight, while angrily demanding authority; Nietzsche and Lawrence, I suspect, can best be viewed in moral politics as authoritarian anarchists.

As writers, too, in their obsessively energetic flow which rarely found a consistent form, they seem inherently contradictory: poet-polemicists, iconoclastic myth-makers, visionaries full of anti-moral moralizings, perhaps equally suggestive and irritating. Both wrote brilliantly, sometimes, though often sliding into a fractured and murky rhetoric of rage. Differences, too, of course: Nietzsche could be far better in argumentative writing—dialectical, complex, ironic—where Lawrence tended to be more bombastic and fundamentalistic. Nietzsche had a powerful sense of scene, felt vision, dramatization, or, especially, human character and relationship.[58] The rhythms and tones of their writings, I suggest, can hardly be separated from their feverish illnesses (damaged brain, damaged lungs); certainly both not only wrote out of illness, alternately pained and euphoric, but *wrote* their illness, as with their very "nauseas" (for the "herd man" and the "mob") and with their very grandiloquentizing of various personal disabilities, including the sexual. (This may be why literal-minded and other moralistic readers, and critics, go so badly wrong with both.) Their disabilities were many. For example, both had periods of disgusting sycophancy (Nietzsche with the Wagners, Lawrence with the Morrells, etc.), and both later took literary revenge. Grievously ill as children, each also obsessively retaliated against mothering women. While the misogyny may have some charm (for the male reader), and Lawrence had great imaginative empathy with women (the majority of his protagonists, and not just the destructive willful witches, were female), Nietzsche's images of women were dominated by a juvenile and impotent cynicism.[59] They had trouble with male friends, too, making great homoerotic demands, insisting that others be followers, then feeling betrayed. The Nietzschean–Lawrencean sexual ambivalences take on monumental shapes, heightened by exacerbated senses of alienation and loneliness. Socially as well as psychologically, then, both wrote as therapy; or, as Lawrence once admitted, "one sheds one's sickness in books."[60] Indeed, self-therapy may be seen as central to their aesthetic credos.

It might be argued also that the blatantly extreme disparities of styles and demands in Nietzsche and Lawrence rather obviate the moralistic warnings of critics against them—the linking with Adolf Hitler, and the like[61]—since the roller-coaster effects, swooping from sensitive tenderness to raging nastiness, often become self-cauterizing, reader-therapeutic. Anyway, dispassionately viewed, both were often pathetic figures, whether in their fantasies of selfish utopias of personal friends (which each proposed in absurd style), or in compulsive wanderings, or in puritanic little economies, or in incompetence with liquor, or in obscurantism about health, or in more-than-invalid irritabilities, or in grandiloquent mythicizing, or in authoritarian posturing. In commonsensical ways, they were often inadequate men, and therefore all the more grotesque in their megalomanias of aristocratic power and force. The recurrent nastiness—for example, Nietzsche wanted to whip women and, apparently, other mediocrities; Lawrence recommended whipping children, and other convicts[62]—hardly qualified as Nietzsche's trumpeted "nobility" and Lawrence's "superiority." Nor did their multiple racist bigotries, demands for caste-rule, sexual denunciations of others and yearnings for apocalyptic destructions. Perhaps worst of all (since we read them, not live with them) there is much crassness, sheer confusion, and bullying and other ugliness in their writings. But "bad motives," both would probably agree as well as demonstrate, at least as much as goodness and love, may make for intelligence and art.

Lawrence and Nietzsche partake of what we may now see as a vestigial but important archetype: the modern rebellious Protestant psychopath as intellectual artist. From whatever perspective one approaches them (except, of course, obtuse piety or righteous dismissal), much will rightly appear inconsistent, obsessional, extreme, raging, ill, perverse. Is this the price that must be paid (to use a proper puritan moral metaphor) for some undeniable power of perception and style and thought? It would seem to be the price they had to pay (not alone among modernists), perhaps not just because insight is costly but because badness and ugliness also inhere in the quest for human truth and salvation. Nietzsche and Lawrence, in their very demand for passion, for intensity and over-reaching, were willing to pay.

A more abstract way of putting this might be that Lawrence and Nietzsche conjoin in being both nihilists and anti-nihilists, extreme aye and nay sayers, however difficult it may be sometimes to tell which is which. Central here seems to be the issue of authority; both acutely insisted that that of Christianity, traditional idealism and morality, rationality, political-moral hierarchy, and even their own pursuits of truth-seeking and art-forming, were grievously in doubt. Both ambivalently demanded counter-authority, legitimizations. (Perhaps authority had to be additionally ambivalent because neither ever commanded much of anything, not just in public roles but even with family, pupils, cultural esteem.) Both piled up fantasy arguments for new authority to replace the slavish and mechanical which, as they saw it, dominated the leaders as well as the masses of modern societies. They radically demanded nothing less than totally new societies and being—rather more than art and discourse can bear.

In brigading Lawrence and Nietzsche, there may be the unintended implication of simple equality. Rather obviously, I think, Lawrence at his best was the superior artist, and also much more acute psychologically. It may be less than accidental that the writings—essays, stories, novels—citing Nietzsche or congruent with the Nietzschean concerns of Will to Power, Dionysian aristocracy, etc., were most often not Lawrence's best. In quality, aesthetic and intellectual, Lawrence elsewhere does better. His best novels—*Sons and Lovers* and *Lady Chatterley's Lover*, his dozen or two best short fictions, and his intense descriptive writings and poems—relate only more distantly to the Nietzschean (and therefore have not been discussed here).

Yet the "last metaphysician," which he certainly was for Lawrence, properly remains a figure to reckon with, perhaps as much for reasons of cultural history and dialectics as for his fractured intellectual suggestiveness. From Lawrence's youth to the present, the Nietzschean provides a locus for the attack on prevailing values, the efforts at "transvaluation," and the dramaturgy of demystification of a nihilistic age.[63] Lawrence, then, with good reason and passion, was not only an English Nietzsche—though certainly that in sensibility—but continued that prophetic matrix. And after all, in a mere century, our culture has not gone clearly beyond the Nietzschean–Lawrencean awareness and difficulties.

# Notes

## Introduction  *Jeffrey Meyers*

1. T. S. Eliot, "Tradition and the Individual Talent," *Selected Essays, 1917–1932* (London, 1932), p. 4.
2. T. S. Eliot, *After Strange Gods* (Charlottesville, Va., 1934), pp. 58–59, 61.
3. T. S. Eliot, "Foreword" (1951) to Martin Jarrett-Kerr, *D. H. Lawrence and Human Existence*, 2nd ed. (London, 1961), p. 10. Eliot also attacked Lawrence in a letter to the *Nation and Athenaeum*, 5 April 1930, p. 11; in his review of *Son of Woman*, *Criterion*, 10 (July 1931), 768–774, where he used Middleton Murry's treacherous book of "destructive criticism" as a stick to beat Lawrence; and in "The Idea of a Christian Society" (1940) in *Christianity and Culture* (New York, 1968), p. 49. Eliot published John Heywood Thomas' "The Perversity of D. H. Lawrence" in *Criterion*, 10 (October 1930), 5–22.
4. See Donald Davie, *A Gathered Church* (London, 1978).
5. T. S. Eliot, "Shakespeare and the Stoicism of Seneca," *Selected Essays*, p. 116.
6. Iris Murdoch, "T. S. Eliot as a Moralist," *T. S. Eliot: A Symposium*, ed. Neville Braybrooke (London, 1958), p. 148.
7. F. R. Leavis, *For Continuity* (Cambridge, England, 1933), p. 158.
8. F. R. Leavis, "Mr Eliot and Lawrence" (1951), *The Achievement of D. H. Lawrence*, ed. Frederick J. Hoffman and Harry T. Moore (Norman, Okla., 1953), pp. 99–101.
9. Anna Balakian, "Influence and Literary Fortune: The Equivocal Junction of Two Methods," *Yearbook of Comparative and General Literature*, 11 (1962), 29.
10. W. Jackson Bate, *The Burden of the Past and the English Poet* (Cambridge, Mass., 1970), p. 3.
11. Harold Bloom, *The Anxiety of Influence* (New York, 1973), p. 5.
12. See, for example, Lawrence's autobiographical essays, "Nottingham and the Mining Countryside," *Phoenix*, ed. Edward McDonald (London, 1936), pp. 133–140, and "Hymns in a Man's Life," *Phoenix II*, ed. Warren Roberts and Harry T. Moore (London, 1968), pp. 597–601.
13. See Rose Marie Burwell, "A Catalogue of D. H. Lawrence's Reading from Early Childhood," *D. H. Lawrence Review*, 3 (1970), 193–324.
14. See Göran Hermerén, *Influence in Art and Literature* (Princeton, 1975), which tries to provide a logical basis for the conditions and measurement of influence.

15  Haskell Bloch, "The Concept of Influence in Comparative Literature," *Yearbook of Comparative and General Literature*, 7 (1958), 35, 37.
16  Ihab Hassan, "The Problem of Influence in Literary History," *Journal of Aesthetics and Art Criticism*, 14 (1955), 73, 75.
17  See Herbert Lindenberger, "Lawrence and the Romantic Tradition," *A D. H. Lawrence Miscellany*, ed. Harry T. Moore (Carbondale, Ill., 1959), pp. 326–341; Graham Hough, *Two Exiles: Lord Byron and D. H. Lawrence* (Nottingham, 1956); Emile Delavenay, *D. H. Lawrence and Edward Carpenter* (London, 1971); L. D. Clarke, "D. H. Lawrence and the American Indian," *D. H. Lawrence Review*, 9 (1976), 305–372; Jeffrey Meyers, *D. H. Lawrence and the Experience of Italy* (Philadelphia, 1982), on Melville, Stevenson and Verga; Henry Gifford, "Anna, Lawrence and the Law," *Critical Quarterly*, 1 (1959), 203–206; Daniel Dervin, "D. H. Lawrence and Freud," *American Imago*, 36 (1979), 95–117; Armin Arnold, *D. H. Lawrence and German Literature* (Montreal, 1963); Jeffrey Meyers, *Painting and the Novel* (Manchester, 1975), pp. 46–82.
18  Lawrence not only followed and developed a tradition but also created one. His positive influence is found in the work of Aldous Huxley, W. H. Auden, Lawrence Durrell, Dylan Thomas and Ted Hughes; in the travel books of Gerald Brenan, Graham Greene, Christopher Isherwood, Jan Morris and Paul Theroux; in the American novels and plays of Sherwood Anderson, Henry Miller, John Steinbeck, Tennessee Williams and Norman Mailer; and in the poetry of William Carlos Williams, Karl Shapiro, Theodore Roethke and Galway Kinnell.

Chapter 1   Lawrence and Blake   *John Colmer*

1  F. R. Leavis, *For Continuity* (Cambridge, England, 1933), p. 113. Compare his later angry response to a British Council pamphlet that stated that "Lawrence's two ancestors are Blake and Whitman" in *D. H. Lawrence: Novelist* (London, 1957), p. 12.
2  Harry T. Moore, *The Life and Works of D. H. Lawrence* (London, 1951), p. 313.
3  Constantine Stavrou, "William Blake and D. H. Lawrence," *University of Kansas City Review*, 22 (1956), 235–240, and Kerker Quinn, "Blake and the New Age," *Virgina Quarterly Review*, 13 (1937), 271–285.
4  Leavis, *For Continuity*, p. 111.
5  Eugene Goodheart, *The Utopian Vision of D. H. Lawrence* (Chicago, 1963), p. 5.
6  Quinn, "Blake and the New Age," p. 275.
7  E. T. [Jessie Chambers], *D. H. Lawrence: A Personal Record*, 2nd ed. (London, 1965), pp. 62–63.
8  Gilchrist describes how a caller at Hercules Buildings found Mr and Mrs sitting in their summer house, "freed from all 'those troublesome disguises' which have prevailed since the Fall. '*Come in!*' cried Blake;

'it's only Adam and Eve, you know!' Husband and wife had been reciting passages from *Paradise Lost*, in character, and the garden of Hercules Buildings had to represent the Garden of Eden." *Life of William Blake*, ed. Ruthven Todd (London, 1942), p. 97. The *Life*, first printed in 1863, was reprinted in 1880 and 1907. This Garden of Eden idyll was discredited by Arthur Symons in *William Blake* (London, 1907), pp. 72–73.

9. Among those who helped to revive interest in Blake at the turn of the century were Ellis, Symons, Selincourt and Yeats.
10. Aldous Huxley, *Point Counter Point* (1928), (Harmondsworth, 1955), p. 108.
11. *A D. H. Lawrence Companion*, ed. F. B. Pinion (London, 1978), p. 100.
12. *Ibid.*, p. 108.
13. D. H. Lawrence, *Letters, 1901–1913*, ed. James Boulton (Cambridge, England, 1979), p. 109.
14. D. H. Lawrence, *Complete Poems*, ed. Vivian de Sola Pinto and Warren Roberts (1964), (London, 1972), p. 183.
15. *Ibid.*, p. 5.
16. Leavis, *For Continuity*, p. 112.
17. D. H. Lawrence, *Phoenix II*, ed. Warren Roberts and Harry T. Moore (London, 1968), pp. 227–237.
18. *The Marriage of Heaven and Hell*, Pl. 3, line 6; "To Thomas Butts," lines 83–88.
19. Lawrence, *Phoenix II*, p. 235.
20. Graham Hough, *The Dark Sun: A Study of D. H. Lawrence* (1956), (London, 1968, p. 223.
21. Parallels noted by Kerker Quinn, "Blake and the New Age," pp. 282–283.
22. D. H. Lawrence, *Lady Chatterley's Lover* (Harmondsworth, 1960), p. 163. In the Foreword by Frieda Lawrence the novelist is reported as saying of the first draft, "they'll say as they said of Blake: It's mysticism, but they shan't get away with it, not this time: Blake's wasn't mysticism, neither is this" (*The First Lady Chatterley*, 1944; Harmondsworth, 1973, p. 10).
23. Goodheart, *Utopian Vision*, p. 35.
24. Colin Clarke, *River of Dissolution: D. H. Lawrence and English Romanticism* (London, 1969), p. 18, and D. H. Lawrence, *Studies in Classic American Literature* (1923), (Harmondsworth, 1971), p. 70.
25. D. H. Lawrence, *Fantasia of the Unconscious* and *Psychoanalysis and the Unconscious* (Harmondsworth, 1971), p. 96.
26. Goodheart, *Utopian Vision*, pp. 104–107.
27. Lawrence, *The First Lady Chatterley*, pp. 156–157.
28. Lawrence, *Phoenix II*, p. 378.
29. Mark Schorer, *The Politics of Vision* (New York, 1946), p. 46.

30  The phrases are quoted by Ian Robinson, "D. H. Lawrence and English Prose," *D. H. Lawrence: A Critical Study of the Major Novels and Other Writings*, ed. A. H. Gomme (Hassocks, Sussex, 1978), p. 13. Robinson defines and illustrates the sense in which Lawrence's prose is "poetic" but he does not explore Lawrence's relation to Blake or other Romantic poets.
31  D. H. Lawrence, *Selected Literary Criticism*, ed. Anthony Beal (1956), (London, 1961), p. 88.

Chapter 2   Lawrence and Carlyle   *Paul Delany*

1  See Harry T. Moore, ed., *D. H. Lawrence's Letters to Bertrand Russell* (New York, 1948), Appendix B and illustration facing p. 88.
2  D. H. Lawrence, *Letters, 1901–1913*, ed. James Boulton (Cambridge, England, 1979), p. 509—hereafter cited as *Letters*, vol. 1.
3  The most detailed previous discussion of the connection between Lawrence and Carlyle is by Edward Alexander, "Thomas Carlyle and D. H. Lawrence: A Parallel," *University of Toronto Quarterly*, 37 (1968), 248–267.
4  E. T. [Jessie Chambers], *D. H. Lawrence: A Personal Record*, 2nd ed. (London, 1965), pp. 101–102.
5  Thomas Carlyle, *Sartor Resartus*, ed. C. F. Harrold (New York, 1937), p. 72—hereafter cited as *Sartor*.
6  Thomas Carlyle, *On Heroes, Hero-Worship, and the Heroic in History* (London, 1840), p. 16—hereafter cited as *Heroes*.
7  D. H. Lawrence, *Phoenix*, ed. Edward McDonald (London, 1936), p. 89.
8  Harold Bloom, *The Anxiety of Influence* (New York, 1975), p. 69—hereafter cited as *Anxiety*.
9  Lawrence, *Phoenix*, 422–423.
10  Thomas Carlyle, *Chartism* (London, 1840), p. 75.
11  Thomas Carlyle, *Past and Present* (London, 1843), p. 255.
12  In modern times, the closest equivalent to these ideals would be found in Japan, where industry is more expressive of feudal or "Samurai" values than in the West (largely because the transition from feudalism to industrialism took place more quickly, and with fewer intermediate stages).
13  D. H. Lawrence, *Women in Love* (Harmondsworth, 1960), p. 242.
14  D. H. Lawrence, *Movements in European History* (London, 1971), p. 309.
15  D. H. Lawrence, *The Plumed Serpent* (New York, 1955), p. 272.
16  Thomas Carlyle, *Shooting Niagara: and After?* (London, 1867), p. 46. Cf. Lawrence, in "Education of the People": "In the afternoon, actual *martial* exercises, swimming, and games, actual gymnasium *games*, but

no Swedish drill. None of that physical-exercise business, that meaningless, vicious self-automatization; no athleticism. Never let physical movement be didactic, didactically performed from the mind" (*Phoenix*, p. 612).

17 Cf. Lawrence's letter to Ernest Collings on the virtues of the unconscious: "I'm like Carlyle, who, they say, wrote 50 vols. on the value of silence" (*Letters*, p. 504).

18 *Froude's Life of Carlyle*, abridged and edited by John Clubbe (Columbus, Ohio, 1979), p. 339—hereafter cited as Froude.

19 D. H. Lawrence, *Letters 1913–1916*, ed. George Zytaruk and James Boulton (Cambridge, England, 1981), p. 307.

20 F. R. Leavis, *D. H. Lawrence: Novelist* (New York, 1969), p. 17. For a contrary view, see Raymond Williams, *Culture and Society* (New York, 1960), p. 199.

21 Jessie Chambers recalls that Lawrence "was loud in his denunciation of Carlyle's affectation of a German style" (*A Personal Record*, p. 101).

22 D. H. Lawrence, "Song of a Man Who Has Come Through," *The Complete Poems*, ed. Vivian de Sola Pinto and Warren Roberts (New York, 1971), p. 250.

## Chapter 3  Lawrence and Ruskin  *George P. Landow*

1 Richard Aldington, *Portrait of a Genius, But . . . The Life of D. H. Lawrence, 1885–1930* (London, 1950), p. 7. Aldington, who was generally hostile and unsympathetic to the Ruskinian element in Lawrence's prose, perceived many such points of influence. In *Portrait of a Genius, But . . .*, he not only saw the resemblance between Lawrence's characteristic inconsistencies and Ruskin's and the equally characteristic polemicism of both men (p. 8), but he also pointed to their shared digressive, heavily symbolic and didactic styles (p. 155). Pointing out that the "dogmatic tone" of Carlyle and Ruskin is "akin" to Lawrence's, Aldington also notes that "both in temperament and opinions he had much in common with Ruskin even down to his inveterate habit of wrangling about personal ideas in terms of a personal symbolism" (p. 38).

2 Keith Alldritt, *The Visual Imaginiation of D. H. Lawrence* (London, 1966), pp. 72–73. Alldritt's valuable chapter "The Tradition of Ruskin," which chiefly concerns Ruskin's influence on *The Rainbow*, makes many fine observations on the way Lawrence used Ruskin and his ideas within the novel, but, unfortunately, because he never looks particularly closely at Ruskin's writings or the ideas which may have attracted Lawrence, he much oversimplifies the complex relationship of the two writers.

3   Few of the writers who make this assertion, however, give any impression of having read Ruskin's once influential writings on politico-economics. Fortunately, recent studies of this portion of Ruskin's work will make future comparison to Lawrence much easier to perform. See James Sherburne, *John Ruskin or the Ambiguities of Abundance* (Cambridge, Mass., 1972) and Alan Lee, "Ruskin and Political Economy: *Unto this Last*," *New Approaches to Ruskin*, ed. Robert Hewison (London, 1981), pp. 68–88.
4   Keith Sagar, *The Art of D. H. Lawrence* (Cambridge, England, 1966), p. 161. The remark that Sagar quotes but does not identify comes from *The Queen of the Air* (1869), Ruskin's imaginative treatise on mythology which would seem to have had a heavy effect on Lawrence's style and method in *Etruscan Places*, *Apocalypse* and many other books.
5   David J. Gordon, *D. H. Lawrence as a Literary Critic* (New Haven, Conn., 1966), p. 3.
6   Arnold Hauser, *The Social History of Art* (New York, 1952), 2. 819–822.
7   Gordon, *Lawrence as a Literary Critic*, pp. 8–9.
8   *Ibid.*, p. 48; see Elizabeth K. Helsinger, "The Structure of Ruskin's *Praeterita*," *Approaches to Victorian Autobiography*, ed. George P. Landow (Athens, Ohio, 1979), pp. 203–231.
9   Gordon, *Lawrence as a Literary Critic*, p. 58; see my *The Aesthetic and Critical Theories of John Ruskin* (Princeton, 1971), pp. 399–420.
10  In the fifth volume of *Modern Painters* (1860), Ruskin argued that "the foolishest misunderstanding" of man possible is that "he has, or should have, no animal nature. For his nature is nobly animal, nobly spiritual—coherently and irrevocably so; neither part of it may, but at its peril, expel, despise, or defy the other. All great art confesses and worships both." Therefore, according to him, "every form of asceticism on one side, of sensualism on the other, is an isolation of his soul or his body" (*Works*, ed. E. T. Cook and Alexander Wedderburn [London, 1903–12], 7.263–264; hereafter cited in text with Arabic volume and page number).
11  Alldritt, *Visual Imagination*, pp. 118–121. Barbara K. Lewalski, *Milton's Brief Epic: The Genre, Meaning, and Art of "Paradise Regained"* (Providence, R.I., 1966), and *Protestant Poetics and the Seventeenth-Century Religious Lyric* (Princeton, 1979), provide a history of the kind of biblical influence upon literary form that Alldritt posits.
12  George P. Landow, *Victorian Types, Victorian Shadows: Biblical Typology and Victorian Literature, Art and Thought* (Boston, Mass., 1980) provides the background in English Victorian biblical interpretation and its literary influence to many of the traditional types and symbols Lawrence employs in *The Rainbow*.
13  D. H. Lawrence, *Twilight in Italy* (London, 1956), p. 22; hereafter cited

in text. Compare his description of Cagliari in the closing pages of the section entitled "The Sea" in *Sea and Sardinia*. Like Ruskin's many descriptions of mountain scenery, both in his autobiographical and art critical writings, this passage takes the form of a sudden sight, a moment of visual perception felt as a moment of spiritual or imaginative vision as well:

> And suddenly there is Cagliari: a naked town *rising* steep, golden-looking, *piled* naked to the sky from the plain at the head of the formless hollow bay. It is strange and rather wonderful, not a bit like Italy. The city *piles up* lofty and almost miniature, and makes me think of Jerusalem: without trees, without cover, rising rather bare and proud, remote as if back in history, like a town in a monkish illuminated missal . . . rather jewel-like: like a rose-cut amber jewel naked at the depth of the vast indenture. The air is cold, blowing bleak and bitter, the sky is all curd. And that is Cagliari. It has that curious look, as if it could be seen, but not entered. It is like some vision, some memory, something that has passed away (emphasis added; D. H. Lawrence, *Sea and Sardinia* [London, 1956], p. 52; hereafter cited in text).

This passage's presentation of a prospect vision and its comparison of that view to both a medieval missal and the New Jerusalem all resemble many parts of *Modern Painters* and *Praeterita*. This Ruskinian prospect vision, one immediately recognizes, derives its energy from its active verbs, but it is not composed in visual terms as is the description of the mountain view from San Tommaso, for Lawrence presents the viewer looking at the scene rather than placing him within it.

14  Another way that Lawrence metamorphoses description into narrative appears in his magnificent opening pages of "San Gaudenzio" in *Twilight in Italy*. There he neither includes a natural element, such as a moving cloud or stream, which moves through the scene to create movement, nor does he, as in the San Tommaso prospect vision, transform static visual elements into kinetic ones to produce the same effect. Rather he presents the transformation of scene in the course of the seasons almost purely in terms of a narrative of changes.

15  For discussions of the expressionistic use of the Pathetic Fallacy in Victorian literature, see H. M. McLuhan, "Tennyson and Picturesque Poetry," *Critical Essays on the Poetry of Tennyson*, ed. John Killham (New York, 1960), pp. 67–85; and Judith T. Christ, *The Finer Optic: The Aesthetics of Particularity in Victorian Poetry* (New Haven, Conn., 1975).

16  A similar use of word-painting appears when Ursula and Skrebensky walk near the corn-stacks and canal in "First Love."

17  Richard Stein, *The Ritual of Interpretation: The Fine Arts as Literature in Ruskin, Rossetti and Pater* (Cambridge, Mass., 1975), p. 53.

18 John Ruskin, *Modern Painters*, IV (Works, 6.35).
19 *Modern Painters*, I (Works, 3.134).
20 Billy T. Tracy, "The Failure of the Flight: D. H. Lawrence's Travels," *Denver Quarterly*, 12 (1977), 205–217, and "'Reading up the Ancient Etruscans': Lawrence's Debt to George Dennis," *Twentieth Century Literaature*, 23 (1977), 437–450, and his 1976 Columbia University PhD disertation, "Coasts of Illusion: The Travel Books of D. H. Lawrence," provide interesting background about Lawrence's use of the tradition of travel writing. Elizabeth K. Helsinger, *Ruskin and the Art of the Beholder* (Cambridge, Mass., 1982) provides a similar discussion of Ruskin in this context.
21 See Erwin Panofsky, "Iconography and Iconology: An Introduction to the Study of Renaissance Art," *Meaning in the Visual Arts* (Garden City, NY, 1955), which originally appeared as an introduction to *Studies in Iconology* (Oxford, 1939).
22 In the third volume of *Modern Painters* (1856), Ruskin argues that "the title 'Dark Ages,' given to the medieval centuries, is, respecting art, wholly inapplicable. They were, on the contrary, the bright ages; ours are the dark ones. . . . We build brown brick walls, and wear brown coats. . . . There is, however, also some cause for the change in our own tempers. On the whole these are much *sadder* ages than the early ones; not sadder in a noble and deep way, but in a dim wearied way,—the way of ennui, and jaded intellect, and uncomfortableness of soul and body" (5.321).
23 John Holloway, *The Victorian Sage: Studies in Argument* (London, 1953), correctly argues that writers in this mode attempt to convince chiefly by poetical or rhetorical means rather than on the basis of logical argumentation, and many of the essays in *The Art of Victorian Prose*, ed. Lionel Madden and George Levine (New York, 1969) contribute to our understanding of what I take to be an identifiable literary genre.
24 George P. Landow, "Ruskin as Victorian Sage: The Example of 'Traffic,'" *New Approaches to Ruskin*, ed. Robert Hewison (London, 1981), pp. 89–91.

Chapter 4   Lawrence and George Eliot   *H. M. Daleski*

1 D. H. Lawrence, "Give Her a Pattern," *Phoenix II*, ed. Warren Roberts and Harry T. Moore (London, 1968), pp. 535–536.
2 Raney Stanford, "Thomas Hardy and Lawrence's *The White Peacock*," *Modern Fiction Studies*, 5 (1959), 19.
3 John Alcorn, *The Nature Novel from Hardy to Lawrence* (London, 1977), p. 81. See too Ross C. Murfin, who states that both George Saxton and Lettie Beardsall are composite portraits, virtually compilations, derived from a number of Hardy characters in each case (*Swinburne*,

Hardy, *Lawrence and the Burden of Belief* [Chicago, 1978], pp. 188–189).
4  E. T. (Jessie Chambers], *D. H. Lawrence: A Personal Record*, 2nd ed. (London, 1965), p. 21
5  George Eliot, *The Mill on the Floss*, ed. Gordon S. Haight (Boston, Mass., 1961), p. 8. All further references are to this edition, designated *MF*. The novel was first published in 1860.
6  D. H. Lawrence, *The White Peacock* (London, 1976), p. 13. All further references are to this edition, designated *WP*. The novel was first published in 1911.
7  Chambers, *A Personal Record*, pp. 97, 98, 103.
8  Cf. George Eliot's own admission in this respect: "My love of the childhood scenes made me linger over them; so that I could not develop as fully as I wished the concluding book in which the tragedy occurs, and which I had looked forward to with attentive premeditation from the beginning" (letter to François D'Albert-Durade, 29 January 1861, *The George Eliot Letters*, ed. Gordon S. Haight [New Haven, Conn. 1954–55], 3.374).
9  The analysis of *The Mill on the Floss* and *The White Peacock* in terms of this pattern in the following section of this paper is based in part on the view of these novels detailed in my book *The Divided Heroine: A Recurrent Pattern in Six English Novels* (New York, 1983).
A similar pattern may be discerned in Hardy's *Tess of the d'Urbervilles*, but—to go by Jessie Chambers—Lawrence's numerous comments on George Eliot and *The Mill on the Floss* and his apparent lack of interest in Hardy when he was writing his first novel suggest it was the earlier writer who held his attention then. It is striking that Jessie Chambers' "account of Lawrence's reading" in the chapter entitled "Literary Formation" in *A Personal Record*, while full of detailed references to a large number of writers and their books, contains only one bare mention of Hardy and makes no reference to a specific work: "Hardy's name had been familiar in our house since childhood days" (p. 110).
10  Chambers, *A Personal Record*, p. 105.
11  D. H. Lawrence, "... Love Was Once a Little Boy," *Reflections on the Death of a Porcupine* (Philadelphia, 1925), p. 183.
12  Letter to Blanche Jennings, 4 November 1908 (D. H. Lawrence, *Letters, 1901–1913*, ed. James Boulton [Cambridge, England, 1979], p. 88).
13  Chambers, *A Personal Record*, pp. 97–98.
14  D. H. Lawrence, *Fantasia of the Unconscious* (1922), (London, 1931), p. 99.

Chapter 5  Lawrence and Hardy *Robert Langbaum*

1  Harold Bloom, *The Anxiety of Influence* (New York, 1973), p. 141. The fact that Lawrence in the *Study* says not a word about Hardy's poetry might be laid to "anxiety of influence" were it not that Hardy's poetry is only a minor influence on Lawrence's, which owes far more to Walt Whitman.
2  D. H. Lawrence, *Study of Thomas Hardy*, first published in *Phoenix*, ed. Edward McDonald (1936), (New York, 1968), p. 480. Lawrence also expressed his admiration for Hardy in many places other than the *Study*, for example: "They are all—Turgenev, Tolstoi, Dostoevsky, Maupassant, Flaubert—so very *obvious* and coarse, beside the lovely, mature and sensitive art of... Hardy" (letter of 27 November 1916, D. H. Lawrence, *Collected Letters*, ed. Harry T. Moore, [New York, 1962]. 1.488).
3  Lawrence, *Letters*, 1.287, 290. "My book on Thomas Hardy ... has turned out," he wrote Amy Lowell on 18 December 1914, "as a sort of Story of My Heart" (1.298).
4  Lawrence, *Phoenix*, p. 444.
5  In *The Sisters*, the name Templeman for Ella's (Ursula's) first lover (the original of Skrebensky in *The Rainbow*) may derive from Lucetta's adopted surname in Hardy's *The Mayor of Casterbridge*.
6  Lawrence, *Phoenix*, pp. 479–480.
7  Mark Kinkead-Weekes, "The Marble and the Statue: The Exploratory Imagination of D. H. Lawrence," *Imagined Worlds: Essays in Honour of John Butt*, ed. Maynard Mack and Ian Gregor (London, 1968), p. 380.
8  Lawrence, *Phoenix*, p. 415.
9  See Charles L. Ross, *The Composition of "The Rainbow" and "Women in Love"* (Charlottesville, Va., 1979), pp. 28–31.
10  D. H. Lawrence, *The Rainbow* (New York, 1968), pp. 1–3.
11  Thomas Hardy, *Tess of the d'Urbervilles*, ed. Scott Elledge (New York, 1979), ch. XXIV, p. 125.
12  Lawrence, *Phoenix*, p. 415.
13  *Ibid.*, p. 441.
14  *Ibid.*, pp. 416–417.
15  Lawrence, *The Rainbow*, p. 437.
16  D. H. Lawrence, *The Complete Short Stories* (New York, 1967), 2.347.
17  Lawrence, *Phoenix*, p. 419.
18  See Michael Millgate, *Thomas Hardy: A Biography* (New York, 1982), p. 295.
19  Hardy, *Tess*, ch. XXXVI, p. 205.
20  Lawrence, *Letters*, 1.273.
21  D. H. Lawrence, *Letters, 1901–1913*, ed. James Boulton (Cambridge, England, 1979), p. 205.

22  Lawrence, *Collected Letters*, 1.282, 281. My quotations are from Moore's edition of the *Letters*, except in note 21 where I quote a letter not in Moore.
23  Lawrence, *Phoenix*, pp. 410–411.
24  Thomas Hardy, *Far from the Madding Crowd* (New York, 1960), ch. XXII, p. 141.
25  Hardy, *Tess*, ch. V, p. 34.
26  Thomas Hardy, *The Return of the Native*, ed. James Gindin (New York, 1969), Book Fourth, ch. III, p. 205.
27  Hardy, *Madding Crowd*, ch. XXVIII, pp. 176, 179, 184.
28  Hardy, *Tess*, ch. VIII, p. 45; ch. XLVII, p. 275. These quotations could also be read as signs of class oppression, but the examples are too extreme to support only that reading.
29  *Ibid.*, ch. X, p. 58; ch. XXVIII, p. 150.
30  *Ibid.*, ch. XXX, p. 161.
31  D. H. Lawrence, *Women in Love* (New York, 1966), ch. XIV, p. 162.
32  Hardy, *Tess*, ch. LVII, p. 318.
33  See, for example, Lascelles Abercrombie's *Thomas Hardy* (New York, 1912), the critical book Lawrence asked to borrow along with Hardy's novels when he was planning his book on Hardy. If we "allegorize the story," writes Abercrombie, "then Tess will be the inmost purity of human life, the longing for purity which has its intensest instinct in virginity; and Alec d'Urberville is 'the measureless grossness and the slag' which inevitably takes hold of life, however, virginal its desires" (p. 149).
34  Thomas Hardy, *Jude the Obscure*, ed. Norman Page (New York, 1978), Part Sixth, vi-2, pp. 263–264; vi-1, p. 261; vi-2, pp. 266–268.
35  Lawrence, *Phoenix*, pp. 506, 508–509.
36  *Ibid.*, p. 488.
37  Hardy, *Tess*, ch. XIX, p. 105.
38  Lawrence, *Phoenix*, pp. 496–497.
39  *Ibid.*, p. 436.
40  *Ibid.*, pp. 439–440, 488–490, 484, 490.
41  Hardy, *Return of the Native*, Book Fourth, ch. I, p. 187.
42  Lawrence, *Phoenix*, p. 420.
43  Hardy, *Tess*, ch. XXX, p. 161; ch. XLI, p. 233.
44  Lawrence, *Women in Love*, ch. XIX, p. 238.

Chapter 6   Whitman and the Poetics of Lawrence   *Roberts W. French*

1  D. H. Lawrence, *Studies in Classic American Literature* (1923), (New York, 1964), p. 171. Further references to this work, abbreviated *SCAL*, will appear in the text.

2   Walt Whitman, *Leaves of Grass*, ed. Sculley Bradley and Harold W. Blodgett (New York, 1973), p. 84. Further references to this edition, abbreviated *LG*, will appear in the text.
3   *The Portable Blake*, ed. Alfred Kazin (New York, 1946), p. 258. The quotation is from "The Marriage of Heaven and Hell."
4   D. H. Lawrence, *Phoenix II*, ed. Warren Roberts and Harry T. Moore (New York, 1978), p. 364. Further references to this work will appear in the text.
5   D. H. Lawrence, *Collected Letters*, ed. Harry T. Moore (New York, 1962), 1.189. Further references to these volumes, abbreviated *CL*, will appear in the text.
6   Huxley's comments appear in his Introduction to D. H. Lawrence, *Letters* (New York, 1932), pp. xxix-xxx.
7   D. H. Lawrence, *Phoenix*, ed. Edward McDonald (New York, 1936), p. 539. Further references to this work will appear in the text.
8   Horace Traubel, *With Walt Whitman in Camden* (New York, 1961), 1.10. Further references to this work will appear in the text.
9   D. H. Lawrence, *Complete Poems*, ed. Vivian de Sola Pinto and Warren Roberts (New York, 1977), p. 522. Further references to this text, abbreviated *CP*, will appear in the text.
10  D. H. Lawrence, *The Symbolic Meaning*, ed. Armin Arnold (New York, 1964), p. 233.
11  E. T. [Jessie Chambers], *D. H. Lawrence: A Personal Record*, 2nd ed. (New York, 1965), pp. 101, 122.
12  Henry David Thoreau, *Walden and Other Writings*, ed. Brooks Atkinson (New York, 1950), p. 86. The chapter is "Where I Lived, and What I Lived For."
13  "The Poet," *Selections from Ralph Waldo Emerson*, ed. Stephen E. Whicher (Boston, Mass., 1960), p. 236.
14  John Middleton Murry, review of *Women in Love*, *Nation and Athenaeum*, 13 August 1921; reprinted in *D. H. Lawrence*, ed. H. Coombes (Harmondsworth, 1973), p. 139.
15  Gay Wilson Allen, ed., *The New Walt Whitman Handbook* (New York, 1975), p. 1.
16  The best-known example of this line of criticism is probably R. P. Blackmur, "D. H. Lawrence and Expressive Form," *Form and Value in Modern Poetry* (Garden City, NY, 1957), pp. 253-267. Henry James' review of *Drum-Taps* may be found in *Walt Whitman*, ed. Francis Murphy (Baltimore, 1970), p. 83.
17  *Walt Whitman*, ed. Murphy, pp. 162-163.
18  A. Alvarez, "D. H. Lawrence: The Single State of Man," *Modern Poetry: Essays in Criticism*, ed. John Hollander (New York, 1968), pp. 294-295.
19  See Jeffrey Meyers, "D. H. Lawrence and Homosexuality," *Homosexuality and Literature* (London, 1977, pp. 131-161.

20  D. H. Lawrence: A Composite Biography, ed. Edward Nehls (Madison, 1957), 1.500–501.
21  See David Cavitch, D. H. Lawrence and the New World (New York, 1969), p. 66.
22  D. H. Lawrence, Apocalypse (New York, 1976), pp. 125–126.

Chapter 7   Lawrence and the Nietzschan Matrix  Kingsley Widmer

1  Most emphatically, of course, with F. R. Leavis, D. H. Lawrence: Novelist (London, 1955) and Thought, Words and Creativity (New York, 1976); on the latter see my "Psychiatry and Piety on Lawrence," Studies in the Novel, 9 (1977), 195–200.
2  A particularly but by no means uniquely egregious example is Richard Swigg, Lawrence, Hardy, and American Literature (London, 1972).
3  For example: Emile Delavenay, D. H. Lawrence and Edward Carpenter: A Study in Edwardian Transition (London, 1971). For some of the relations with Carlyle, see several of the studies cited in note 7 below, and the interesting discussion of the tradition of English "imagination" in John Brian, Supreme Fictions (Montreal, 1974).
4  Among many sentimental examples, see Harry T. Moore, The Priest of Love: A Life of D. H. Lawrence (New York, 1974) and Phillip Callow, Son and Lover: The Young D. H. Lawrence (New York, 1975). I have discussed a number of Lawrence biographies in "Profiling an Erotic Prophet," Studies in the Novel, 8 (1976), 234–243.
5  For Whitman, see Studies in Classic American Literature (1923) (New York, 1953), ch. 12, and for a negative comment on Blake, p. 82; for a more mixed comment on Blake, see Phoenix, ed. Edward McDonald (London, 1936), p. 560. There are others.
6  See Martin Green, The von Richthofen Sisters (New York, 1974). While I think much of Green's argument as to the influence of Frieda on Lawrence's "Lebensphilosophie" is patently wrong (and some of the evidence is indicated below), his more general emphasis on the ideological cast and subterranean traditions of sensibility (rather than just "sources" and "influences") is importantly appropriate.
7  An early discussion here, a liberal polemic but still useful, is Eric Bentley, A Century of Hero-Worship (New York, 1944), pp. 221–253. Other discussions of Lawrence and Nietzsche include: H. Steinhauer, "Eros and Psyche: A Nietzschean Motif in Anglo-American Literature," Modern Language Notes, 64 (1949), 217–228—though brief, acute on several points; Kingsley Widmer, The Art of Perversity: D. H. Lawrence's Shorter Fictions (Seattle, 1962), pp. 241–242, and, more indirectly, throughout; Eugene Goodheart, The Utopian Vision of D. H. Lawrence (Chicago, 1963),

whose scattered comments loosely draw ideological parallels between the two; Ronald Gray, *The German Tradition in Literature, 1871–1945* (Cambridge, England, 1965), pp. 328–354, who draws sweeping similarities, centering on *Women in Love*; David S. Thatcher, *Nietzsche in England, 1890–1914* (Toronto, 1970), rather misleadingly only mentions Lawrence in passing; Patrick Bridgwater, *Nietzsche in Anglosaxony* (Leicester, 1972), pp. 104–109, gives a competent brief summary of some of the influence; Emile Delavenay, *D. H. Lawrence, The Man and His Work: The Formative Years, 1885–1919* (London, 1972), disapprovingly catalogues, without analysis, many of the Nietzschean similarities, often via other writers; John B. Humma, "D. H. Lawrence as Friedrich Nietzsche," *Philological Quarterly*, 53 (1974), 110–120, reasonably emphasizes the continuity and similarity of thought; Eleanor Green, "Blueprints for Utopia: The Political Ideas of Nietzsche and D. H. Lawrence," *Renaissance and Modern Studies*, 18 (1974), 141–161, points up similarities, particularly with the "leadership novels" (which I modify below); John Burt Foster, Jr., *Heirs to Dionysus: A Nietzschean Current in Literary Modernism* (Princeton, 1981), pp. 180–255, points up relations between *Twilight in Italy* and *Twilight of the Idols* but is merely ingenious with *Women in Love* and unincisive with the later novels. Usually without additional citation, I have drawn on several of the above, and have extended the arguments into other areas. Though this list is incomplete, clearly there is a long-sustained and informed tradition of commentary on Lawrence as an English Nietzsche. Yet, apparently for covert academic ideological reasons, much of this is ignored, or even denied, in a large part of Anglo-American literary study. This anti-intellectual parochialism might itself be a curious subject.

8 Ford Madox Ford, *Return to Yesterday* (London, 1931), p. 392. A sensible comment on the passage is provided by James Boulton, "Introduction," D. H. Lawrence, *Letters, 1901–1913* (Cambridge, England, 1979), p. 9.

9 E. T. [Jessie Chambers], *D. H. Lawrence: A Personal Record*, 2nd ed. (London, 1965), p. 120. The passage has been previously discussed by Bentley, Steinhauer *et al.* Bridgewater, *Nietzsche in Anglosaxony*, p. 104, suggests that Lawrence read the Zimmern translation of *Beyond Good and Evil* in 1908 (I would guess 1909), and other works shortly after, which were locally available in translation. While Lawrence knew German, and was later relatively fluent—see Armin Arnold, *D. H. Lawrence and German Literature* (Montreal, 1963)—it seems likely that most of his Nietzsche was in English, with later German tags picked up from Frieda. While the translations used were most likely those collected in the Levi edition (London, 1908–13), my quotations below are taken from later more accurate translations since my main issues are not source-texts but intellectual parallels, ideological similarities and sensibilities.

10  In D. H. Lawrence, *Complete Short Stories* (London, 1955), 1.6. There are various other Nietzsche references in Lawrence, such as the innocuous one in *Collected Letters*, ed. Harry T. Moore (New York, 1962), 1.204.
11  D. H. Lawrence, *The Trespasser* (1912) (London, 1955).
12  Reprinted in Lawrence, *Phoenix*, p. 304.
13  *Ibid.*, pp. 490–492. Elsewhere in his meandering ruminations around Hardy, Lawrence shrewdly rejects Nietzsche's late doctrine of "eternal recurrence" by insisting "each cycle is different. There is no real recurrence" (*Phoenix*, p. 461). This may imply the sensible moral as well as logical objection to the doctrine.
14  Egbert, the Georgian aesthete centering this awkward story, seems admirable but lacks an "acrid courage, and a certain will-to-power." He ends by revealing his (and the English genteel cultural tradition's) longing for self-destruction. See my *Art of Perversity*, pp. 13–22. I will not repeat here my analyses of many of the shorter fictions.
15  D. H. Lawrence, *The Rainbow*, (1915), (London, 1950), p. 283.
16  *Ibid.*
17  *Ibid.*, pp. 460–461. I am giving only a few representative examples.
18  D. H. Lawrence, *Phoenix II*, ed. Warren Roberts and Harry T. Moore (New York, 1970), p. 94.
19  *Ibid.*, p. 103.
20  D. H. Lawrence, *Women in Love* (1920), (New York, 1960), p. 170. Similar redefinitions can also be found scattered in Nietzsche—see the sources cited in note 47.
21  *Ibid.*, p. 255.
22  *Ibid.*, pp. 245–246.
23  *Ibid.*, pp. 286ff. There are many more similar dialectics.
24  D. H. Lawrence, *The Lost Girl* (1920), (London, 1950), p. 57. In context, this applies to the "slaves" in the twentieth-century mining town but also to the explicitly "slavish" submission of Alvina to the dark mastery of her lover.
25  Lawrence, *Complete Short Stories*, 3.701–721; Widmer, *Art of Perversity*, pp. 78–81.
26  D. H. Lawrence, *Reflections on the Death of a Porcupine* (London, 1934), p. 145.
27  "The final aim is not *to know*, but *to be*" (D. H. Lawrence, *Fantasia of the Unconscious* [New York, 1933], p. 60). It is variously repeated elsewhere—central valuation in Lawrence, and in Nietzsche. For Nietzsche's concept of Will to Power see the references cited in note 47. Neither writer is always consistent about such terms and ontology.
28  Lawrence, *Complete Stories*, 3.589, for the specific reference to Nietzsche. Moore summarizes the biographical background; see *Priest of Love*, pp. 381 and 386–387.

29 Other examples of the Lawrence projection into military-aristocrat heroes include Captain Hepburn of the novella "The Captain's Doll," a ragged (contra-Leavis) but suggestive attempt to portray a considerately dominant-male marriage morality, and Count Dionys (add to the discussion of the Dionysian, below) in the novella "The Ladybird," a stickily mythological ghost story of *Übermensch* romantic adultery and aristocratic anarchism. The contrasting effete intellectual Phillip of "The Border Line" is not only of a piece with the similar character in "Smile" and "The Last Laugh," both trivial *romans à clef*, but of the recurrent figures of cerebral wickedness in the better tales, such as the intellectual clergyman (Massey) in "The Daughters of the Vicar" and Bertie in "The Blind Man."

30 Widmer, *Art of Perversity*, ch. 2, "The Demon Lover."

31 D. H. Lawrence, *Aaron's Rod* (1922), (London, 1950). But take a point where Lawrence seems to diverge from Nietzsche, such as "Homage ... is just a convention and social trick" (p. 164), and repeatedly demonstrates it in the fiction; Nietzsche, good middle-European, repeatedly praises social obeisance and would happily enforce it as an expression of the *"instinct for rank"* (*Beyond Good and Evil*, trans. Walter Kaufmann [New York, 1966], p. 212, and see other comments in Part Nine, "What Is Noble"). Yet Lawrence's intermittent emphasis on the "aristocratic principle" ends up with a similar demand, in spite of his lower-class cynical wisdom.

32 Lawrence, *Aaron's Rod*, pp. 78 and 301.

33 *Ibid.*, pp. 135, 255 and 311. There is also some racist ranting, pp. 103ff.

34 *Ibid.*, p. 293; preceding quote, p. 27.

35 *Ibid.*, p. 294; see Lawrence's preface to Dostoyevsky, "The Grand Inquisitor," reprinted *Phoenix*, pp. 283–291, for other praise of authoritarianism. For Nietzsche on "socialism" as an extension of the moral sickness of Christianity, see *The Will to Power*, trans. Walter Kaufmann and R. J. Hollingdale (New York, 1968), pp. 77–78, and many similar remarks elsewhere. The attack in the novel on "idealism" undoubtedly intends it in a very specific sense as well—Platonism. Nietzsche, of course, mounted it in *The Birth of Tragedy*, especially against the figure of Socrates in the later sections, and repeated it in later writings. For Lawrence, idealism connected with Plato marks false authority and impotence—effete aristocrat–Platonist husband Boris in "The Ladybird," impotent aristocrat–Platonist husband Clifford in *Lady Chatterley's Lover*, are representative. Given the exalted status of Plato in late-Victorian thought, Lawrence's non-positivist villainizing of Plato would also certainly have to derive from Nietzsche.

36 Lawrence, *Aaron's Rod*, pp. 303, 307, 310.

37 No attempt is made here to cover all the fictions, much less all the writings, only selections in a rough chronological order.

38  See Moore, *Priest of Love*, pp. 293–352.
39  D. H. Lawrence, *Kangaroo* (1923), (London, 1950).
40  See my "The Pertinence of Modern Pastoral: The Three Versions of *Lady Chatterley's Lover*," *Studies in the Novel*, 5 (1973), 298–313, revised part reprinted in *The Edge of Extremity* (Tulsa, Okla., 1980), ch. 3, the only detailed analysis I am aware of.
41  Lawrence, *Kangaroo*, pp. 180 and 233.
42  *Ibid.*, pp. 323 and 277.
43  *Ibid.*, p. 291.
44  *Ibid.*, p. 324.
45  *Ibid.*, p. 305. Nietzsche has similar historical examples of "great men," though the language of both sometimes suggests more vitalistic or spiritual heroes.
46  For Nietzsche on *ressentiment* as the envious "morality" of the weak, see *On the Genealogy of Morals*, trans. Walter Kaufmann and R. J. Hollingdale (New York, 1969), pp. 36ff. As indicated in the biographical comparisons, section III, below, there were good reasons for a similar vice in the two writers.
47  Lawrence, *Kangaroo*, pp. 309 and 324. For recent discussions of Nietzsche's similar Will to Power, see Walter Kaufmann, *Nietzsche: Philosopher, Psychologist, Antichrist*, 4th ed. (Princeton, 1974), pp. 178ff, and the qualifications of J. P. Stern, *Nietzsche* (Hassocks, Sussex, 1978), pp. 76ff. Arthur C. Donato provides a commonsensical discussion in *Nietzsche as Philosopher* (New York, 1965).
48  Lawrence, *Kangaroo*, pp. 361 and 366. Something similar to the doctrine above, a kind of vitalist evolution, also appears in the description of the New Mexico scene in the final section of *St Mawr*.
49  D. H. Lawrence, *The Plumed Serpent* (1926) (New York, 1951). *Thus Spake Zarathustra* in *The Portable Nietzsche*, trans. and ed. Walter Kaufmann (New York, 1968), pp. 112–439.
50  Lawrence, *The Plumed Serpent*, pp. 55 and 128. I forbear from citing the many silly discussions of the novel. The "morning star" also appears in *Zarathustra*, and many other parallels could be drawn with Nietzsche's most ambitious mythopoeic work, including the synthetic rhetoric (neither at his best), and the lack of human character development—unusual in Lawrence but not in Nietzsche (cf. Stern, *Nietzsche*, pp. 102ff). I am inclined to see this novel as a considerable aberration from Lawrence's more usual extreme individualism (as in the previous two novels), which is the more important tradition for Lawrence. And for Nietzsche. For example, I suspect that John Carroll is right to see (in contrast to commentators like Kaufmann) Max Stirner crucially behind Nietzsche. See his introduction to *The Ego and His Own* (1844), trans. Steven Byington (London, 1971), pp. 24–25, and annotations throughout; also, John Carroll, *The Break-Out from the Crystal Palace*

Notes to pages 126–128

(London, 1974). But though Stirner (like Lawrence) savages sexual renunciation in his insistence on the ultimacy of individual being, Carroll would have to miss any parallel with Lawrence: see his snide comments on the "delusional" view of Lawrencean sex in *Puritan, Paranoid, Remissive: A Sociology of Culture* (London, 1977), pp. 41–42. Behind Stirner one might find certain Enlightenment libertarian sexual psychologies, such as that of Charles Fourier. Steinhauer, above, also related Nietzschean–Lawrencean views to the French Enlightenment, by way of Heine. While it is usual to see Schopenhauer (also read by Lawrence) behind Nietzsche's view of Will—"My body and my will are one" (discussed by Ronald Hayman, *Nietzsche: A Critical Life* [New York, 1980], p. 72)—there may be other heritages to these essential Nietzsche–Lawrence tropes: speculatively, Fourier, Stirner, Nietzsche, Lawrence, with subterranean Enlightenment traditions, recurrent paganizing and radical Protestantism.

51  I may have borrowed the epithet from Kenneth Rexroth.

52  See notes 6 and 7 to my essay on *Lady Chatterley's Lover*, *Studies in the Novel*, p. 310. Norman Mailer discussed it in *The Prisoner of Sex* (New York, 1971) in his continuation of the tradition.

53  Lawrence, *The Plumed Serpent*, p. 132. While the phrases supposedly apply to "bad" murderers, the giveaway sadism in their execution—"the clutching throb of gratification as the knife strikes in and the blood spurts out!" (p. 133)—confirms that the nastiness is merely ritualized in the Dionysian "good" viciousness of Cipriano and Ramón.

54  For other final explorations of late values, see Donald Gutierrez, *Lapsing Out: Embodiments of Death and Rebirth in the Last Writings of D. H. Lawrence* (Cranbury, NJ, 1980).

55  The point was apparently first passingly made by Eric Bentley, *Century of Hero-Worship*, p. 233, who also noted some similar ambivalences of character. I have extended the argument, drawing on the previously cited biographies of Lawrence and Nietzsche and, especially, on Ronald Hayman, *Nietzsche: A Critical Life*, though some of the interpretive points there are more implicit than avowed. I am not, of course, arguing complete similarity. The two differed in sexuality (Hayman, *Nietzsche: A Critical Life*, p 64, concludes that Nietzsche had an "abnormally low" sexual drive; it may have been total impotence, in spite of Wagner's suspicion that he masturbated too much; Lawrence apparently was not fully impotent until his forties, and, of course, positive sexuality takes a much greater role for him). They also partly differed in class origins (minister's son v. coalminer's son), in education (classical academic philology v. grammar school–teacher training), in scene and country, and in social state during their main writing periods (isolated professor v. married writer in bohemia), in disease (syphilis v. tuberculosis, though both were persistent bronchial cases), in respon-

siveness (generally reticent v. mercurial), even in hirsuteness (overgrown military mustache v. trimmed full beard), etc., yet many fundamental similarities seem evident—to use current jargon, we may speak of a *mentalité*.

56  Nietzsche, *Zarathustra*, p. 124; Lawrence, *Phoenix*, p. 726. There are many similar statements.
57  Lawrence, *Aaron's Rod*, p. 303; and see the biographies.
58  I can only suggest, not demonstrate, the issue here, and grant that the differences included those of languages, educations and their subcultures' pro-and-anti-philosophical biases, as well as differences in talents.
59  See, for example, Nietzsche's vitriolic attacks on feminism, *Beyond Good and Evil*, pp. 162–170, and the juvenile epigrams on women scattered through Part Four of the same book. Lawrence had the more complex and varied view of women; for a monograph responsively attempting to present a fuller positive view, see Charles Rossman, "'You are the call and I am the answer': D. H. Lawrence and Women," *D. H. Lawrence Review*, 8 (1975), 255–328. While there has been much discussion of the issue recently, most of it is not very good, as with the thin excursus of Carol Dix, *D. H. Lawrence and Women* (London, 1980), and most of the essays in *Lawrence and Women*, ed. Anne Smith (New York, 1978). Certainly Lawrence's views show some variation, though unusual perceptiveness, sexual ambivalence, the linking of women to willful idealism and a final insistence on male dominance, are among the constants.
60  Lawrence, *Collected Letters*, 1.234 (October 1913, long before his more serious illnesses).
61  For one of many examples with Lawrence, see the inaccurate and confused study of Frank Kermode, *D. H. Lawrence* (New York, 1973).
62  In a conversation many years ago, Eric Bentley granted that Kenneth Burke may have been right in suggesting that he should have understood Zarathustra's "When thou goest to woman, take thy whip" as sexual rather than punitive, but it still looks like impotent sadism to me. The Lawrence demand that children be whipped appears in some ramblings on education (in spite of the earlier revulsion he showed via Ursula in the school scene in *The Rainbow*, though she ends up feeling that she has to beat the boy).
63  See, for example, Martin Heidegger, *Nietzsche*, vol. I, trans. D. T. Krell (New York, 1979), from whom I also draw several points on the Will to Power; or, more recent work, Jacques Derrida, "Nietzsche's Styles," *Spurs/Eperons* (Chicago, 1979), a rather ponderous unadmitted joke which re-mystifies Nietzsche (except for his "venomous anti-feminism," p. 57) in order to escape the demystification.

# Index

Abercrombie, Lascelles, *Thomas Hardy*, 142 n33
Alcorn, John, *The Nature Novel from Hardy to Lawrence*, 53–54
Aldington, Richard, *Portrait of a Genius, But*, 35, 136 n1
Alldritt, Keith, *The Visual Imagination of D. H. Lawrence*, 35, 37, 136 n2
Allen, Gay Wilson, 100
Alvarez, A., 103
Arnold, Matthew, 15, 47
Austen, Jane, *Emma*, 51; *Mansfield Park*, 51; *Pride and Prejudice*, 51

Balakian, Anna, 2, 6
Bate, Walter Jackson, *The Burden of the Past*, 2–3
Baynes, Godwin, 109
Bennett, Arnold, 4
Bentham, Jeremy, 26
Berryman, John, *Dream Songs*, 102
Blake, William, 3, 5, 6, 9–20, 93, 115, 134 n22, 144 n5; "The Clod and the Pebble," 12; "Infant Joy," 12; *Jerusalem*, 16, 19; *The Marriage of Heaven and Hell*, 11, 13, 17, 92; *Milton*, 19; *Pencil Drawings*, 11; Prophetic Books, 14, 16, 18, 19; *Songs of Innocence* and *Songs of Experience*, 11, 12; "The Tyger," 12; *Vala, or The Four Zoas*, 18
Bloch, Haskell, 3–4
Bloom, Harold, 9; *The Anxiety of Influence*, 3, 24, 33, 53, 64, 69
Brontës, 4, 82, 115, 117; Charlotte, *Jane Eyre*, 21, 52; Emily, 11; *Wuthering Heights*, 52
Browning, Robert, 91
Burrows, Louie, 33, 76
Byron, George Gordon, Lord, 4

Carlyle, Jane, 23
Carlyle, Thomas, 3, 6, 15, 21–34, 37, 46, 47, 115, 136 n1, 144 n3; *Chartism*, 26; *The French Revolution*, 29; *Heroes and Hero-Worship*, 23, 24, 26; *Latter-day Pamphlets*, 27; "The Nigger Question," 25; *Past and Present*, 26, 32; *Sartor Resartus*, 22, 25, 31; *Shooting Niagara*, 27–28, 30–31
Carpenter, Edward, 4, 115
Chambers, Jessie (E. T.), *D. H. Lawrence: A Personal Record*, 10, 11, 22, 54–55, 56, 60, 116–117, 140 n9
Clarke, Colin, 16
Coleridge, Samuel Taylor, 15, 17–18
Colmer, John, 6, 9–20
Cooper, James Fenimore, 4
Corke, Helen, 12

# Index

Daleski, H. M., 6, 7, 51–68
Dante, 2, 7
Delany, Paul, 6, 21–34
Dickens, Charles, 4, 52, 82; *Oliver Twist*, 51

Eliot, George, 3, 51–68, 69, 115, 117, 140 n8; *Adam Bede*, 52; *Middlemarch*, 52, 57, 76; *The Mill on the Floss*, 6, 52, 53, 54–62, 64, 66, 140 n9
Eliot, T. S., 4, 7, 98, 132 n3; *After Strange Gods*, 1–2; "Tradition and the Individual Talent," 1; *The Waste Land*, 102
Emerson, Ralph Waldo, 108; "The Poet," 98

Fielding, Henry, 56
Flaubert, Gustave, 116; *Madame Bovary*, 21
Ford, Ford Madox, 116
French, Roberts W., 6, 7, 91–114
Freud, Sigmund, 4, 7, 10, 16, 17, 100, 116
Froude, James Anthony, *Life of Carlyle*, 31

Galsworthy, John, 22
Garnett, Edward, 21, 22
Gilchrist, Alexander, *Life of William Blake*, 10–11, 133–134 n8
Ginsberg, Allen, 110
Goodheart, Eugene, 9–10, 15–16
Goodman, Paul, 110
Gordon, David, *D. H. Lawrence as a Literary Critic*, 35–36
Green, Martin, *The von Richthofen Sisters*, 144 n6

Hardy, Thomas, 3, 4, 5, 7, 21, 22, 69–90, 115, 139 n3, 141 n2; *The Dynasts*, 71; *Far From the Madding Crowd*, 72, 75, 76, 78–79, 81, 87–88; *Jude the Obscure*, 53–54, 75, 76, 77, 83–88; *The Mayor of Casterbridge*, 141 n5; *The Return of the Native*, 72, 73–75, 78, 81, 86, 87, 88; *Tess of the d'Urbervilles*, 53, 71, 72–73, 75, 76, 78, 79–82, 85–88, 140 n9, 142 n33; *The Woodlanders*, 87
Hassan, Ihab, 4
Hauser, Arnold, *The Social History of Art*, 36
Hegel, Georg Wilhelm, 23
Hermerén, Göran, *Influence in Art and Literature*, 132 n14
Holloway, John, *The Victorian Sage*, 47, 139 n23
Hough, Graham, 14, 17
Huxley, Aldous, 94; *Point Counter Point*, 11

Ibsen, Henrik, 22

James, Henry, 22, 103
Jennings, Blanche, 12, 32
Johnson, Samuel, *The Rambler*, 2–3
Joyce, James, 7, 69

Keats, John, 4

# Index

Kinkead-Weekes, Mark, 71, 72

Landow, George P., 6–7, 35–50
Langbaum, Robert, 6, 7, 69–90
Lawrence, D. H.
  attitude to predecessors, 4–8, 36; Blake, 10–11, 12–13, 115; Carlyle, 21–22, 25, 33, 136 n17, 136 n21; George Eliot, 52, 54–55; Hardy, 69–77, 84–89; Nietzsche, 117, 121; Whitman, 91–92, 97, 99–100, 104, 109, 115
  background: intellectual, 1–2, 4, 28, 115–116; religious, 2, 5, 6, 14, 24, 37, 50, 95; travels, 28, 29, 30, 44–45
  characterization, 19–20, 54–55, 57–60, 62–68; duality in, 52, 57–60, 62–68, 75; Nietzschean, 111–112; unconscious in, 71, 72, 75, 77, 82, 85, 89–90
  ideas:
    art, 36, 43–45, 95, 100; novel, 71–72, 95; political: anti-democratic, 118–120, 123–125, authoritarian, 24–29, 123, 124–125, 128, 129–131, 147 n35, Nietzschean, 118–119; prophetic, 5, 6, 14, 50, 92–99, 116, 127, 128, 131; sexual, 5, 6, 7, 16–17, 20, 23, 52–53, 67, 70–73, 86, 97, 108, 111, homosexual, 4, 109–110, 119, 124, 128, male-female polarity, 17, 57, 71, 75–76, 78, 85, 87–88, 119–120, 122, 126–127, 150 n59; social, 5, 6, 15–16, 18, 26–30, anti-Christian, 118–119, 121–123, 130, Darwinist, 5, 73, 116, misanthropic, 94, 98, 127
  influences on Lawrence, 2–8, 9–10, 21, 33, 35–38, 52–53, 57, 69, 91–92, 117–121, 131; influence of Lawrence, 133 n18
  poetry: autobiographical, 100–101; death theme, 111–114; free verse, 19, 101–102; incompleteness, 102–103; style, 5–6, 11–13, 19, 91, 96, 99–103
  prose, 5, 13–14, 18, 32, 33, 37, 135 n30; descriptive, 38–48, 72–73; emblems in, 44, 49–50; pathetic fallacy in, 41–42
  relation to literary tradition, 37–38, 115, 139 n20; to the Bible, 14, 37, 97, 137 n12
  technique of composition, 21
  *Works*
  Books:
    *Aaron's Rod*, 24, 122–123, 125, 147 n31
    *Amores*, 101
    *Apocalypse*, 7, 113–114
    *Etruscan Places*, 35
    *Fantasia of the Unconscious*, 17, 67, 146 n27
    *The First Lady Chatterley*, 17
    *Kangaroo*, 4, 24, 123–126
    *Lady Chatterley's Lover*, 1, 4, 6, 7, 15, 25, 51, 67, 87, 124, 131, 147 n35
    *Last Poems*, 111
    *Letters*, 32, 59, 76–77, 94, 95, 100, 101, 103, 108, 109, 112
    *Look! We Have Come Through!*, 6, 92, 111
    *The Lost Girl*, 120, 146 n24
    *Love Poems and Others*, 12

*The Man Who Died*, 4, 14, 25, 127
*Mornings in Mexico*, 47
*Movements in European History*, 24
*The Paintings of D. H. Lawrence*, 11
*Pansies*, 13
*The Plumed Serpent*, 6, 14, 15, 24, 25, 29, 126–127, 149 n53
*The Rainbow*, 4, 6, 7, 16, 21, 37, 40–42, 49–50, 51, 57, 67, 70, 71, 72, 73, 74, 76, 78, 89, 117–118, 138 n16, 150 n62
*St Mawr*, 148 n48
*Sea and Sardinia*, 6, 44–46, 138 n13
*The Sisters* (draft novel), 71, 76, 141 n5
*Sons and Lovers*, 6, 7, 10, 55, 57, 67, 68, 76, 78, 86, 117, 118, 131
*The Symbolic Meaning*, 97
*The Trespasser*, 117
*Twilight in Italy*, 6, 39–40, 42–43, 47, 48, 138 n14, 145 n7
*The White Peacock*, 6, 7, 11, 53–60, 62–68, 139 n3
*Women in Love*, 6, 7, 15, 16, 17, 18, 23, 26–27, 57, 67, 71, 76, 77–80, 81–82, 85, 88–90, 109–110, 118–120, 124, 145 n7

Essays:
  "Aristocracy," 13
  "Art and Morality," 95
  "The Crown," 13, 92–93
  "Edgar Allan Poe," 16
  "Education of the People," 24, 135–136 n16
  "Foreword to *Women in Love*," 18, 119
  "Give Her a Pattern," 52
  "Introduction to These Paintings," 97
  "Morality and the Novel," 95
  "The Novel," 96, 97
  "Obscenity," 13
  "Preface to *Chariot of the Sun* by Harry Crosby," 99
  "Preface to *Collected Poems*," 101, 102
  "Preface to *New Poems*," 19, 96, 97
  "Review of *Georgian Poetry: 1911–1912*," 117
  "Review of *Pedro de Valdivia* by R. B. Cunninghame Graham," 30
  "The State of Funk," 108
  "Study of Thomas Hardy," 6, 7, 25, 54, 69, 70–77, 82, 84–90, 117, 141 n1, 141 n3, 146 n13
  "The Two Principles," 13–14
  "Whitman," 91–92, 100, 107, 110
  "Why the Novel Matters," 96

Poems:
  "The Ass," 12
  "Bavarian Gentians," 111
  "Being Alive," 95
  "The Body of God," 102, 106–107
  "Future States," 28–29
  "Glimpses," 98

"Healing," 106
"Michael Angelo," 11–12
"New Eve and Old Adam," 12
"Retort to Whitman," 100
"Shadows," 111
"The Ship of Death," 111, 112
"Song of a Man Who Has Come Through," 33–34, 105
"Song of Death," 112
"Ten Months Old," 12
"Terra Incognita," 106
"Tragedy," 98
"What Have They Done to You?" 98
Stories:
"The Blind Man," 74
"The Border Line," 121, 122
"The Captain's Doll," 146–147 n29
"England, My England," 117, 146 n14
"The Ladybird," 147 n29, 147 n35
"A Modern Lover," 117
"None of That," 120
Lawrence, Frieda, 3, 7, 76, 116, 122, 124, 134 n22, 145 n9
Leavis, F. R., *D. H. Lawrence: Novelist*, 2, 32, 133 n1; *For Continuity*, 2, 9, 13; *The Great Tradition*, 2, 115
Lewis, Wyndham, 116
Lowell, Robert, *Notebooks*, 102

Marx, Karl, 116
Melville, Herman, 4
Meredith, George, 12, 91
Meyers, Jeffrey, 1–8, *D. H. Lawrence and the Experience of Italy*, 4
Michelangelo, *The Creation of Adam*, 12
Milton, John, 93
Montaigne, Michel de, 48, 100
Moore, Harry T., *The Life and Works of D. H. Lawrence*, 9
Morrell, Ottoline, 101, 129
Murdoch, Iris, 2
Murry, John Middleton, 99, 121

Newton, Isaac, 13
Nietzsche, Friedrich, 3, 4, 5, 7, 10, 16, 115–131, 144–145 n7, 145 n9, 146 n10, 146 n13, 146 n27, 146 n28, 148 n45, 149 n55, 150 n63; *The Antichrist*, 4; *Beyond Good and Evil*, 145 n9, 147 n31, 150 n59; *The Birth of Tragedy*, 147 n35; *The Genealogy of Morals*, 118, 148 n46; *Thus Spake Zarathustra*, 122, 126, 128, 148 n50, 150 n62; *Twilight of the Idols*, 145 n7

Patmore, Coventry, 51
Pinion, F. B., 12
Plato, 147 n35

# Index

Pound, Ezra, 7; *Cantos*, 1, 102; *Hugh Selwyn Mauberley*, 116, 123
Powys, J. C., 116

Quinn, Kerker, 9, 10

Reynolds, Sir Joshua, 43
Rilke, Rainer Maria, 16
Robinson, Ian, 135 n30
*The Rubaiyat of Omar Khayyam*, 11
Ruskin, John, 3, 4, 6–7, 15, 35–50, 136 n1, 136 n2, 137 n3, 137 n4, 138 n13; *Modern Painters*, 36, 38–40, 42, 44, 46, 137 n10, 139 n22; *Praeterita*, 36, 42; *The Seven Lamps of Architecture*, 38; *The Stones of Venice*, 38, 40, 42; "Traffic," 50
Russell, Bertrand, 21, 24

Sagar, Keith, *The Art of D. H. Lawrence*, 35, 137 n4
Santayana, George, 103
Schopenhauer, Arthur, 7, 149 n50
Schorer, Mark, *The Politics of Vision*, 18
Shakespeare, William, 2; *Macbeth*, 76
Shaw, George Bernard, 22, 116
Shelley, Percy Bysshe, 11, 17–18, 93
Stanford, Raney, 53
Stavrou, Constantine, 9, 133
Stein, Richard, 43
Sterne, Laurence, 82
Stevens, Wallace, 107
Stevenson, Robert Louis, 4
Stirner, Max, 148–149 n50
Strindberg, August, 22

Thackeray, William Makepeace, *Vanity Fair*, 51–52, 76
Thoreau, Henry David, 47; *Walden*, 98
Tolstoy, Leo, 4, 7; *Anna Karenina*, 71–72
Traubel, Horace, *With Walt Whitman in Camden*, 95, 100, 104, 108

Verga, Giovanni, 4

Wagner, Richard, 7, 116, 117, 129, 149 n55
Weber, Max, 119
Whitman, Walt, 3, 4, 7, 10, 91–114, 115, 141 n1; *Drum-Taps*, 103; *Leaves of grass*, 92, 94, 95, 96, 98, 99, 100–101, 102, 107, 108, 110, 113, 114; "Out of the Cradle," 111; "The Sleepers," 102; "Song of Myself," 102, 105, 111; "When Lilacs Last in the Dooryard Bloom'd," 111
Widmer, Kingsley, 6, 115–131
Williams, Raymond, 15
Williams, William Carlos, *Paterson*, 102

Wordsworth, William, 4, 17, 46, 69, 73, 82; "Resolution and Independence," 12, 77, 89

Yeats, William Butler, 18, 116